She Shall Be Called Woman

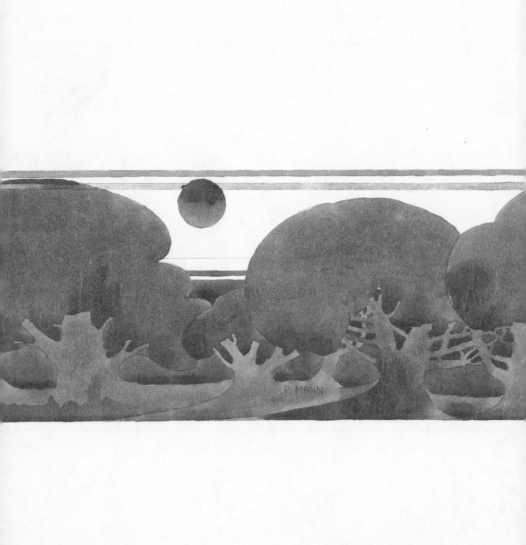
P. MANN

She Shall Be Called Woman

Oscar W. McConkie

Bookcraft
Salt Lake City, Utah

Library of Congress Catalog Number: 79-53830
ISBN 0-88494-380-1

First Printing, 1979

Lithographed in the United States of America
PUBLISHERS PRESS
Salt Lake City, Utah

Contents

Preface

Life was not meant to be easy, and it is not. The same prophet who told us "men [and women] are that they might have joy" cautioned us to expect opposition. The joy comes partly from surmounting the opposition.

For each individual the problems are different, depending on factors too numerous to mention. One of these factors is a person's sex. A woman's problems will differ from a man's simply because of her differing roles in life.

As with us all, a woman gains greater happiness and peace when she understands and accepts her true calling as a woman and all that it implies. In today's world, persistent and strident voices constantly assail a woman's ears with philosophies and counsel which challenge principles and positions once thought fundamental. The same voices mingle with other, quieter ones to deplore past treatment of women and call for reform. How far should one go? What constitutes reform of evil, what renunciation of good? In the hustle and the hassle there is danger that those who lack understanding will surrender to the loudest voices.

The LDS woman frequently cannot remain unaffected by the polarization on this issue. It is for her principally that I have written this book. Its design is to trace briefly the eternal history and principles to which she is committed by conviction and covenant; to show that women's depressed conditions in past eras are one facet of the apostasy from gospel truth; and to provide answers and motivations which will help to sustain her in her "normal" problems and frustrations of life, as well as to help combat the arguments that would threaten her true, long-term interests.

In the process I seek to demonstrate that, notwithstanding past and present defects in attitudes, there is a basic equality between man and woman in all things that truly count. Such things are governed by the spirit, by the heart. As the Lord told the prophet Samuel, "Look not on his countenance, or on the height of his stature; . . . for the Lord seeth not as man seeth; for the man looketh on the outward appearance, but the Lord looketh on the heart." Indeed, it is in the things of the spirit and the rewards resulting from righteousness that we find the most meaningful dimension of equality among humankind.

While I alone take responsibility for the contents of this book, I am grateful to several people who have read the manuscript and offered helpful comments and suggestions. I express appreciation particularly to my wife, Judith, to my daughter Ann Boyden, to my daughter-in-law Carol, and to Marian Lindsay and Moana Bennett for their valued opinions, assistance, and encouragement during the preparation of the manuscript. My thanks go also to Merle D. Bryner and Cathy DeGooyer for typing the manuscript and for their observations and comments. I am especially grateful to my brother Bruce R. McConkie for his careful reading of the text and for his suggestions.

1

Eternal Attributes of Women

Women had an existence long before there was a woman on the earth. Mortality is but a phase of immortality; human beings have no starting place and no stopping place. Nor is immortality a gift reserved for men and women alone, since every living thing is immortal. Even the earth itself, quickened with celestial glory, is an immortal globe. (See D&C 93:29; Moses 3:5; D&C 29:22-25; D&C 77:1; 88:16-19, 25-26.)

A First Presidency of the Church wrote of the premortal existence of the spirit children of God the Father. Presidents Joseph F. Smith, John R. Winder and Anthon H. Lund said: "All men and women are in the similitude of the universal Father and Mother, and are literally the sons and daughters of Deity," the "offspring of celestial parentage." ("The Origin of Man," in Joseph Fielding Smith, *Man: His Origin and Destiny* [Deseret Book Co., 1969], pages 351, 355.)

These spirit beings, the children of exalted parents, looked like mortal men and women; however, their spirit bodies were made of a more refined substance than the elements of mortal bodies. (See Ether 3:16; D&C 131:7-8.) God the Father begat spirit children in his image and in the image of our mother in heaven.

Prophets inspired by the Holy Ghost have made references to our premortal existence. To Jeremiah the Lord said, "Before I formed thee in the belly I knew thee; and before thou camest forth out of the womb I sanctified thee, and I ordained thee a prophet unto the nations." (Jeremiah 1:5.) Job tells us that "the sons of God shouted for joy" at a time prior to the creation of the earth. (Job 38:7.) The apostle Paul received the same inspiration and spoke of "the whole family in heaven." (Ephesians 3:15.)

There was a family in heaven that existed before the world was made. In the words of Brigham Young, "The Father actually begat the spirits, and they were brought forth and lived with Him." (*Journal of Discourses*, 26 volumes [London: Latter-day Saints' Book Depot, 1854-86], 4:218.) The Lord said that he "looked upon the wide expanse of eternity, and all the seraphic hosts of heaven, before the world was made." (D&C 38:1.) We were all there.

"The pre-existent life was thus a period — undoubtedly an infinitely long one — of probation, progression, and schooling. The spirit hosts were taught and given experiences in various administrative capacities. Some so exercised their agency and so conformed to law as to become 'noble and great'; these were foreordained before their mortal births to perform great missions for the Lord in this life. (Abraham 3:22-28.)" (Bruce R. McConkie, *Mormon Doctrine*, 2d. ed. [Bookcraft, Inc., 1966], page 590.)

We *are* individuals, then, not founded in mortality but added upon by mortality. This earth life does not create personality; it merely modifies it.

The essence of a woman, therefore, is her spirit, and spirits entering into mortality possess distinctive attributes, capabilities, and predispositions. "The same variety that we see in the works of God, that we see in the features, visages and forms, exists in the spirits of men." (Brigham Young, *Journal of Discourses*, 11:305.)

Certainly it is reasonable to assume that God's spirit children developed talents in that state of their progression. God has said in our day that "to every man is given a gift by the Spirit of God." (D&C 46:11.) Several types and kinds of endowments were pursued and developed in our pre-earth life.

When we come into mortality, we bring the talents, capacities, and abilities acquired by obedience to law in our prior existence. Mozart composed and published sonatas when but eight years of age because he was born with musical talent. Melchizedek came into this world with such faith and spiritual capacity that "when a child he feared God, and stopped the mouths of lions, and quenched the violence of fire." (Genesis 14:26, Inspired Version.)

[Bruce R. McConkie, *Conference Report,* April 1974, page 103; see also *Ensign,* May 1974, page 73.]

Our personalities, then, are in substantial measure fashioned prior to our births. Mortal birth "is the process by which we bring from premortality to mortality the traits and talents acquired and developed in our long years of spirit existence. It is the process by which a mortal body is created from the dust of the earth to house an eternal spirit offspring of the Father of us all." (Bruce R. McConkie, "The Salvation of Little Children," *Ensign,* April 1977, page 3.)

Female spirits were born into female bodies. Male spirits were born into male bodies.

One of God's divine purposes was to "prove them herewith" that they "who keep their first estate shall be added upon." (Abraham 3:25-26.) That is, part of the plan of God is to allow personality modification and further development in the flesh. Through this experience the children hope to become like their celestial parents and inherit the celestial kingdom. (See D&C 132:19-22.)

To become like one's celestial parents one must acquire and develop their characteristics and attributes; or, as Peter puts it, "be partakers of the divine nature." (See 2 Peter 1:4.) Both sexes are designed with and share equally the ability to manifest all of the attributes of God. Compassion, courage, knowledge, faith, justice, mercy, truth, and love are all scripturally documented attributes of God.

Both men and women are to make God's nature their own, but while both may sing the same song, they do not sing the same part. For example, examine love.

Love is an attribute of God that both men and women share. It is everywhere in the universe — in all things, which have their being from the bounty and generosity of God's creative love and which in return obey the law of love. It seems to fall into the sphere of the emotions and the will, rather than into the sphere of perception and knowledge. Godly love does not possess the object loved, but rather seeks to benefit it. Therefore, the lover wishes and seeks for the well-being of the beloved and gains happiness and joy through the happiness and welfare of the beloved. This love can find satisfaction in the contemplation of the beloved's beauty or goodness. Such love is devoid of selfish desires. Sexual love, on the other hand, is sometimes called the "love of desire" to signify that it is a love born of selfish desire. Godly love seeks the welfare of the beloved.

Love is a thing of the spirit as well as of the body. It is thus unlike other passions that humans share with animals. One is called piggish when he has an excessive appetite for food or drink. One is called a jackal when he is a coward. But when one's love becomes great, one is lifted to acts of devotion and sacrifice which exemplify the best in humans.

A mother's love is as unique an expression of her womanly characteristics as a father's love is an expression of his characteristics as a man.

Mother love exemplifies godly love and is a distinguishing characteristic of worthy motherhood, which is an inherent ability of women. When the Lord made provision for motherhood to go to women, he prepared them for this role. They had a model in their celestial mother. A superlative Latter-day Saint, Eliza R. Snow, penned these lines during the lifetime of the Prophet Joseph Smith:

> In the heavens are parents single?
> No; the thought makes reason stare!
> Truth is reason, truth eternal
> Tells me I've a mother there.
>
> When I leave this frail existence,
> When I lay this mortal by,
> Father, Mother, may I meet you
> In your royal courts on high?
> Then, at length, when I've completed
> All you sent me forth to do,
> With your mutual approbation
> Let me come and dwell with you.
>
> ("O My Father," *Hymns*, number 138.)

Women are endowed with a special ability to love their offspring. This endowment is necessary in keeping the family — the basic unit of society — together. Even if it is only in women's propensity to engage in mother love, that very natural inclination is uniquely feminine. Mother love is a manifestation of inherent ability and talent with which women were endowed. This gift of God, the natural tendency toward which was developed in the presence of a celestial mother, is a natural and superior way that God has to bring his children back into his presence.

Mother love is not the only unique attribute of women, however. My experience as a missionary and as a mission president has shown me women's great sensitivity to spiritual truths and has led me to the same conclusion that Brigham Young reached when he said: "The men are... more inclined to reject the Gospel than the women. The women are a great deal more inclined to believe the truth than the men; they comprehend it more quickly, and... are... easy to teach." (*Journal of Discourses,* 14:120.) This shrewd judge of human nature observed, "Woman is altogether of a finer nature, and has stronger moral inclinations." Of man he says, "He is by nature coarser and more prone to... wickedness." (*Journal of Discourses,* 18:233.)

While these statements suffer the exceptions of all generalizations, analysis in our day tends to verify Brigham Young's observations: The general Church missionary committee has advised me that approximately 65 percent of convert baptisms are female and approximately 35 percent are male. And this is after special programing to bring families into the Church as units. This ratio also reportedly holds true with percentages of male and female Church members.

The talent to recognize and accept truth is a wonderful gift among the many gifts bestowed by God. Everyone is given some gifts. The Lord said to Joseph Smith: "To some is given one, and to some is given another, that all may be profited thereby. To some it is given by the Holy Ghost to know that Jesus Christ is the Son of God.... To others it is given to believe on their words, that they also might have eternal life if they continue faithful." (D&C 46:12-14.)

The ministry of the Lord demonstrated the ability of some to accept his message while others rejected it. When Jesus said to the Jews, "I am the good shepherd" (John 10:14), his hearers understood that he was equating himself with the shepherd spoken of in Psalm 23. But they did not want to accept such oblique statements. They complained, "If thou be the Christ, tell us plainly."

"Jesus answered them, I told you, and ye believed not.... Ye believe not, because ye are not of my sheep, as I said unto you. My sheep hear my voice, and I know them, and they follow me." (John 10:24-27.) The Jews had an intellectual appreciation of what he had said, as they demonstrated by their charge, "Thou, being a man, makest thyself God." (John 10:33.) What was obviously missing in these Jews was the ability to believe the testimony of Jesus. Some had, as did Peter, the talent to believe, "Thou art the Christ, the Son of the Living God." (Matthew 16:16.) Most, however, had not developed this talent and remained unbelieving.

Women seem to be more blessed with this talent and bring a deeper sensitivity with them into mortality. President Harold B. Lee related a story that President David O. McKay told of a good man, but of a more sensitive woman. The man was a General Authority, an able business executive. His son worked as a switchman on a railroad that went up Emigration Canyon to the mines east of Salt Lake City, Utah. He was found crushed to death under a train, and no one knew how it had happened. The mother was overly concerned about the circumstances of the death and was not comforted.

After some weeks, the son appeared to his mother. He comforted her, saying: "Mother, I've been trying to get to Father to tell him it was just an accident. I had thrown the switch and was running to catch on to the handle bars, but my foot tripped against a root at the side of the rail and I was thrown underneath the train. . . . I've been trying to get to Father, but he's too busy at the office. I can't reach him." He told the mother he was happy and she was greatly consoled.

President McKay was concerned that the father was so busy with daily tasks that "spiritual forces" were "not able to reach him." The mother, however, was more spiritually attuned and able to receive her son's message. ("Qualities of Leadership," [Address delivered at the Latter-day Saint Student Association Convention, August 1970], page 5.)

It is regrettable when a person consciously assumes so much of the daily affairs of the world that a deeply rooted sensitivity to spiritual things is forsaken. Of course, it is possible to modify natural characteristics, and some persons prefer to live so as to change these characteristics. By imitating masculine ways females may assume male nuances, and by conscious or unconscious selection they may modify their personalities. Some modern radical feminists seem to become anti-feminine, and males who assume female nuances may become anti-masculine. If either men or women lose their sensitivity to things spiritual, they lose one of God's greatest gifts.

Are there relationships between sensitivity and femininity other than the inherent sensitivity to things spiritually discerned? What of a woman's role as a mother? Besides mother love, does she have any inherent characteristics that peculiarly fit her for this role?

To what extent are male and female differences the result of the eternal attributes and natures with which men and women are born? To what extent are they the result of individual acquirement in this life?

To explore these questions we must look to the most basic of eternal units: the family. The human family, according to Rousseau, is "the most ancient of all societies and the only one that is natural." The family fulfills a natural need: "Therefore shall a man leave his father and his mother, and shall cleave unto his wife: and they shall be one flesh." (Genesis 2:24.) To survive, the human infant requires years of care. The family exists as a stable organization to serve this purpose. Without the family, an alternative social unit would be necessary to satisfy this natural need. As the scriptures and prophets have defined it, a family consists of husband and wife and their offspring. What of the unique roles each fills?

First, the prophets have taught us that "the character of our lives in the spirit world has much to do with our disposition, desires and mentality here in mortal life. The spirit influences the body to a great extent." (Joseph Fielding Smith, *Doctrines of Salvation*, 3 volumes [Bookcraft, Inc., 1954-1956], 1:60.)

Men and women, then, bring into mortality gifts that may be alike diffused in both. In addition, God, knowing their talents, may have foreordained them to specific callings.

> To carry forward his own purposes among men and nations, the Lord foreordained chosen spirit children in pre-existence and assigned them to come to earth at particular times and places so that they might aid in furthering the divine will. These pre-existence appointments, made "according to the foreknowledge of God the Father" (1 Pet. 1:2), simply designated certain individuals to perform missions which the Lord in his wisdom knew they had the talents and capacities to do. . . .
>
> By their foreordination the Lord merely gives them the opportunity to serve him and his purposes if they will choose to measure up to the standard he knows they are capable of attaining. . . .
>
> Moses taught that the whole host of spirits born in the lineage of Jacob were before appointed to come through that chosen line. (Deut. 32:7-8.) It was because of their pre-existent training, election, and foreordination that Christ was able to say of certain chosen ones, "My sheep hear my voice, and I know them, and they follow me." (John 10:27.)
>
> There is scriptural record of many other instances of specific foreordination. . . . Mary, the mother of our Lord, was before named for her sacred mission (1 Ne. 11:18-20; Mosiah 3:8; Isa. 7:14), . . .
>
> In pre-existence, before Jacob or Esau were born as mortal beings, the Lord decreed, "The elder shall serve the younger." (Rom. 9:10-12.) [Bruce R. McConkie, *Mormon Doctrine*, pages 290-91.]

More basic than personalities, talents, or foreordination to callings, however, are inherent characteristics of men and women. Men beget and women bear children, for instance.

Women's dispositions, desires, and abilities were somewhat set in our former existence. They developed through many ages to play their incomparably important part in God's plan. There is a reason why astute observers refer to "the refining feminine touch — physical, mental, moral, spiritual touch — [that] purifies and blesses men and boys.... When the Lord... gave the sacred honor and glory of motherhood to women, he divided... the blessings of life...." (Hugh B. Brown, *Continuing the Quest* [Deseret Book Co., 1961], page 6.)

It is woman's unique responsibility to bear children. She is biologically prepared for her function of motherhood. She has the exclusive anatomical facilities: after her egg is fertilized, the new life is cradled and nurtured in her womb. It is through her blood and water and labor that birth is accomplished. Her whole emotional system is inextricably connected with this life-making process. From the moment the umbilical cord is cut and the new-born child takes suck, the mother is uniquely and intimately involved in sustaining the life she has in large measure created. No wonder she is emotionally, mentally, and physically better able to express love to the offspring than anyone else.

The cumulative wisdom of the law, expressed in the English common law and in statutes, has ever been to the effect that children of a tender age are better placed with their mothers in the event of a broken family, and this is for the welfare of the children.

Motherhood is natural and good. It is a God-given instinct to which all nature bears witness. How instinctively a mother bird looks after her brood and feeds them! How anxiously she teaches them to fly and to fend for themselves! How fearlessly she flies to their protection! It is nature's way.

Other talents too are required by a successful mother. Are these talents innately feminine; or are they acquired and developed through a woman fulfilling her assigned role? Experience and reason would suggest that a man too could develop the patience, the long-suffering, the unselfishness, the ability to sense the proper teaching moment, and other characteristics associated with successful motherhood. However, in light of the revealed truth regarding one's development in a pre-earth life, and accepting the perfect nature and planning of our Father in heaven, it seems natural to accept that, as well as those for feeding, protecting, and teaching offspring, other superior child-rearing talents may have had elsewhere a beginning.

The fact that we cannot give a definitive answer as to whether these talents are innate or learned does not mean that they are not innate. Why shouldn't God prepare his children for their especial and peculiar roles in this earth life? If we clearly bring characteristics with us into this mortal sphere, it is reasonable to regard the application of this principle as broad. Some innate talents and characteristics are, then, uniquely feminine.

With special gifts come special responsibilities, and it is my observation that fulfillment of these responsibilities takes patience and selflessness. Worthy motherhood and unselfishness seem near synonyms. It is the ordinary experience to remember one's mother as unselfish.

At a family reunion, President Marion G. Romney related the adventure of his family fleeing northern Mexico before the armies of Pancho Villa. His mother, Artemesia Redd Romney, and her seven children crossed the Mexican border into Texas with one trunk containing all their worldly goods they could take. It was a struggle to reestablish the family, even after the husband and father was able to join them. It was difficult to provide the necessities of life, and there were few extras and no luxuries. President Romney recalled, "When something special came along, an apple, an orange, or some candy, Mother never did want any." This is a typical example of the sacrifice and selflessness of motherhood.

There are other special gifts and accompanying responsibilities that attend women.

I think that the mark of a true saint is compassion, a character attribute that both women and men should develop but which in general seems to come more naturally to women. It is a vital part of the gospel of Christ and consists in having sorrow for the sufferings of one's fellowmen; in having pity and sympathy for them; and in exhibiting mercy, tenderness, and kindness toward them.

Jesus set the perfect example. James said, " . . . the Lord is very pitiful, and of tender mercy." (James 5:11.) That we should be like him in this is a basic New Testament concept: "Be ye all of one mind, having compassion one of another, love as brethren, be pitiful, be courteous." (1 Peter 3:8.)

Solomon particularly associated compassion and mercy as virtues of womankind. He said, "She stretcheth out her hand to the poor; yea, she reacheth forth her hands to the needy." (Proverbs 31:20.)

Women seem to exemplify compassion and are generally more tenderhearted than men. The Prophet Joseph Smith specifically said that woman's disposition toward this great virtue is a gift of God and is according to nature:

> It is natural for females to have feelings of charity and benevolence. You are now placed in a situation in which you can act according to those sympathies which God has planted in your bosom. . . . (Joseph Smith, *History of The Church of Jesus Christ of Latter-day Saints,* ed. B. H. Roberts, 7 volumes [Salt Lake City: The Church of Jesus Christ of Latter-day Saints, 1932-51], 4:605-607.)

Compassionate service was the charter of the chief auxiliary organization in the Church, the Female Relief Society. Joseph Smith made this entry in his journal on March 24, 1842:

> I attended by request, the Female Relief Society, whose object is the relief of the poor, the destitute, the widow and the orphan, and for the exercise of all benevolent purposes. Its organization was completed this day. . . . There was a very numerous attendance at the organization of the society, and also at the subsequent meetings, of some of our most intelligent, humane, philanthropic and respectable ladies and we are well assured from a knowledge of those pure principles of benevolence that flow spontaneously from their humane and philanthropic bosoms, that with the resources they will have at command, they will fly to the relief of the stranger, they will pour in oil and wine to the wounded heart of the distressed; they will dry up the tears of the orphan and make the widow's heart to rejoice.
>
> Our women have always been signalized for their acts of benevolence and kindness. (Joseph Smith, *History of the Church,* 4:567.)

Women have a responsibility not only to retain those talents and characteristics they brought to this earth but also to add to them.

In the several areas I have classified as especially or uniquely feminine, women are seemingly endowed with special talents. Men cannot raise up and demand equal talents.

Men and women should be equal under the law, but the law cannot make them the same. This is also true for sexual roles. The male who begets a child is not superior to the female who bears it.

There is a difference. At the very least there is a physical difference, and differences should be recognized, even in the law that is established to serve each in his or her capacities. Civil law cannot change that which has been decreed and developed from before the beginning of earth life. Fulfillment as a man or woman on earth comes in developing and adding to the natural endowments, including the innate masculine and feminine propensities.

Before the world was, there were diversities in individuals and talents and roles. It is to this world that we come to be "added upon."

2

Added Upon

God himself," the Prophet Joseph Smith says, "finding he was in the midst of spirits and glory, because he was more intelligent, saw proper to institute laws whereby the rest could have a privilege to advance like himself. The relationship we have with God places us in a situation to advance in knowledge. He has power to institute laws to instruct the weaker intelligences, that they may be exalted with himself, so that they might have one glory upon another, and all that knowledge, power, glory, and intelligence, which is requisite in order to save them in the world of spirits." (Joseph Smith, *Teachings of the Prophet Joseph Smith* [Deseret Book Co., 1938], page 354.)

We are given a glimpse into this pre-earth existence through Father Abraham's recorded vision:

> Now the Lord had shown unto me, Abraham, the intelligences that were organized before the world was; and among all these there were many of the noble and great ones;
>
> And God saw these souls that they were good, and he stood in the midst of them, and he said: These I will make my rulers; for he stood among those that were spirits, and he saw that they were good; and he said unto me: Abraham, thou art one of them; thou wast chosen before thou wast born.

> And there stood one among them that was like unto God, and
> he said unto those who were with him: We will go down, for there
> is space there, and we will take of these materials, and we will
> make an earth whereon these may dwell;
> And we will prove them herewith, to see if they will do all
> things whatsoever the Lord their God shall command them;
> And they who keep their first estate shall be added upon.
> (Abraham 3:22-26.)

Having been given this perception of where we came from, we are
helped to understand why we are here. We are fulfilling our Father's
plan. The plan of salvation, through which we as God's spirit children
can progress to the high state of exaltation enjoyed by our heavenly
parents, is contained in the laws, ordinances, principles, and doctrines
of the gospel. Training for eventual salvation began for each person at
the birth of his spirit. Following a long period of premortal, probationary schooling, this earth was created to be a place where the hosts of
spirits who kept their first estate might come; receive mortal bodies,
and undergo further testings and trials. (See Moses 4:1-4; Abraham
3:22-28.)

What is the purpose of our mortal existence? Why are we here?
Before the creation of this world God said, "We will prove them
herewith." (Abraham 3:25.) We are here to be "added upon," to have
glory added upon that which we gained as spirit children. (See Abraham 3:26.) We have our respective assigned parts in carrying the
great plan forward. Some of those responsibilities come to us because
of our unique missions as either male or female. In the furthering of
God's purposes, Adam and Eve were placed on the earth as the first of
the human family. "And the first man of all men have I called Adam,
which is many," the Lord says. (Moses 1:34; see also Moses 3:7, 6:45;
Abraham 1:3; 1 Nephi 5:11; D&C 84:16.) That is, Adam was placed on
earth as the first of the human family and given a name which signifies
"many" as pertaining to the greatness of the posterity which would
flow from him. Eve as the first woman on the earth became the mother
of the whole human race. Her name signifies "mother of all living."
(See Moses 4:26.) We and all others born on this earth share this same
ancestry. "He (Adam) is the father of the human family, . . . [the] head
of the human family." (Joseph Smith, *Teachings of the Prophet Joseph
Smith,* page 157.)

Birth is the process by which the spirit children of celestial parents
come into this mortal sphere. As it was in our premortal existence, so it
is in mortality. By the ordained procreative process a body is provided,
but this body is made from the dust of this earth, that is, from the

natural elements of this temporal sphere. Three things are necessary to effect every mortal birth: water, blood, and spirit — the same elements found in every rebirth into the fellowship of God's kingdom.

The scriptures refer to Adam as "the son of God." "And this is the genealogy of the sons of Adam, who was the son of God, with whom God, himself, conversed." (Moses 6:22.) A First Presidency statement of 1909, signed by Joseph F. Smith, John R. Winder, and Anthon H. Lund, had this to say:

> The doctrine of the pre-existence... shows that man, as a spirit, was begotten and born of heavenly parents, and reared to maturity in the eternal mansions of the Father, prior to coming upon the earth in a temporal body to undergo an experience in mortality. It teaches that all men existed in the spirit before any man existed in the flesh, and that all who have inhabited the earth since Adam have taken bodies and become souls in like manner.
>
> It is held by some that Adam was not the first man upon this earth, and that the original human being was a development from lower orders of the animal creation. These, however, are the theories of men. The word of the Lord declares that Adam was "the first man of all men" (Moses 1:34), and we are therefore in duty bound to regard him as the primal parent of our race. It was shown to the brother of Jared that all men were created in the *beginning* after the image of God; and whether we take this to mean the spirit or the body, or both, it commits us to the same conclusion: Man began life as a human being, in the likeness of our heavenly Father.
>
> True it is that the body of man enters upon its career as a tiny germ embryo, which becomes an infant, quickened at a certain stage by the spirit whose tabernacle it is, and the child, after being born, develops into a man. There is nothing in this, however, to indicate that the original man, the first of our race, began life as anything less than a man, or less than the human germ or embryo that becomes a man. (James R. Clark, *Messages of the First Presidency*, 6 volumes [Bookcraft, Inc., 1970], 4:205.)

Moses' account of the creation of Eve is manifestly figurative.

> And I, the Lord God, caused a deep sleep to fall upon Adam; and he slept, and I took one of his ribs and closed up the flesh in the stead thereof; and the rib which I, the Lord God, had taken from man, made I a woman, and brought her unto the man. And Adam said: This I know now is bone of my bones, and flesh of my flesh; she shall be called Woman, because she was taken out of man. Therefore shall a man leave his father and his mother, and shall cleave unto this wife; and they shall be one flesh. (Moses 3:21-24.)

This clearly is a manifestation of truth. God did create woman. She is one flesh with her husband. They are bone of each other's bone and flesh of each other's flesh. They should cleave unto one another. God did bring them together. Moses was wholly successful in expressing the true concept. His successful communication was partially dependent upon his skillful use of speech. Moses used figures of speech to transmit his information. He used words and phrases that literally denoted one object to suggest an understandable idea. Men and women are one; that is, they are created out of the same element and are created for each other and God's purposes. They are one flesh.

A modern scriptural scholar, Elder Bruce R. McConkie, has made it clear that Eve was placed on earth through the same process of birth as was Adam. "[Eve] . . . was placed on earth in the same manner as was Adam, the Mosaic account of the Lord creating her from Adam's rib being merely figurative." (Bruce R. McConkie, *Mormon Doctrine,* page 242.)

Birth into this life is a great blessing. It provides opportunities for further eternal advancement. Since Adam and Eve, all who have been born into the world have come as offspring of mortal parents, excepting only the Lord Jesus, who came into the world as the son of a mortal mother and an immortal father. (See 1 Nephi 11:13-21.) Christ is the Only Begotten of the Father. (See Moses 5:9; John 1:18, 3:16.) This means that he is the only Son of the Father in the flesh.

Since "God . . . brought [Eve] unto the man" (Genesis 2:22), we have ever since had the instruction of that moment: "Therefore shall a man leave his father and his mother, and shall cleave unto his wife: and they shall be one flesh." (Genesis 2:24.) Marriage was thus ordained of God from the beginning of earth life.

God not only brought the man and the woman together for this first marriage but he performed the ceremony:

> Marriage as established in the beginning was an eternal covenant. The first man and the first woman were not married until death should part them, for at that time death had not come into the world. The ceremony on that occasion was performed by the Eternal Father himself whose work endures forever. It is the will of the Lord that all marriages should be of like character, and in becoming "one flesh" the man and the woman are to continue in the married status, according to the Lord's plan, throughout all eternity as well as in this mortal life. (Joseph Fielding Smith, *Doctrines of Salvation,* 2:71.)

Since this first wedding ceremony was performed before the Fall, while Adam and Eve were immortal, it can be said with certainty that the marriage was intended to last forever. In addition, as President Joseph Fielding Smith stated, God's "work endures forever." Adam and Eve's marriage was to be everlasting.

When Eve was presented to Adam, he said, "This [woman] is now bone of my bones, and flesh of my flesh." (Genesis 2:23.) From this we understand that they had become one: this union was to be permanent. The Savior confirmed this doctrine when he reminded the Jews: "For this cause shall a man leave father and mother, and shall cleave to his wife: and they twain shall be one flesh. Wherefore they are no more twain, but one flesh." (Matthew 19:5-6.) The Lord's own words once again confirm that marriage is a God-ordained institution.

Our Lord's apostles promulgated his teaching in this matter. Paul taught that "neither is the man without the woman, neither the woman without the man, in the Lord." (1 Corinthians 11:11.) Having created male and female in his own image (see Genesis 1:27), the Lord said, "It is not good that the man should be alone; I will make him an help meet for him." (Genesis 2:18.) This is further affirmation that marriage has the approbation of God. This dictum goes beyond simply affirming the rightness of marriage. It signifies the wrongness of man remaining single under normal circumstances. It was not good for man to be alone in the beginning, and it never was and never will be good for man to be alone.

God said he would give a "help meet" for man. (Genesis 2:18.) "Help meet" does not mean servant. "Help meet" in this context means a companion through whom the fulness of the purposes of the Lord can be accomplished. The Lord's purposes for man and woman are inextricably connected through mortal life and into eternity. As the apostle Paul indicated, neither can be fulfilled without the other.

"The Prophet Joseph [Smith] taught that 'marriage was *an institution of heaven,* instituted in the Garden of Eden; [and] that it ... should be solemnized by the authority of the everlasting priesthood.' " (Joseph Fielding Smith, *Doctrines of Salvation,* 2:70.)

The scriptures say that "Adam began to till the earth, and to have dominion over all the beasts of the field, and to eat his bread by the sweat of his brow ... and Eve, also, his wife, did labor with him." (Moses 5:1.) This is the type of companionship envisioned in the scriptures; a companionship where couples work out their salvation together in things of the spirit and stand shoulder to shoulder in overcoming the world. The instructions to our first parents imply a husband-and-wife relationship that is a fulfilling and eternal partnership. They work together, are one flesh, and must remain together if they are to achieve unity with the Lord.

When God the Father performed the marriage of Adam and Eve, it was meant to establish a perfect and celestial pattern for their children throughout the generations of time. A man or woman who chooses to remain "separately and singly" (D&C 132:17) throughout eternity will lose the greatest blessings that the Lord has prepared for them that love him. It is an inherent, God-given desire that causes a normal man and a normal woman to leave father and mother when they become mature and to marry. They follow the examples set before them and cleave unto each other in a husband-wife companionship and union that in all righteousness should be equal and endure forever. It is the will of the Lord that the marriage of our parents, Adam and Eve, be our proto-type.

It should be remembered that when Adam and Eve were born on the earth it was a terrestrial sphere in paradisiacal glory. (The Tenth Article of Faith tells us that the earth will be "renewed and receive its paradisiacal glory.") Our first parents were placed on earth as immortal beings. Their coming was the crowning event of the creation. At that time immortality reigned supreme. (See 2 Nephi 2:22.) There was no death and no mortality. Blood did not flow in their veins, for they were not yet mortal, and blood is an element that pertains exclusively to mortality. (See Leviticus 17:11; see also Joseph Fielding Smith, *Man: His Origin and Destiny,* pages 362-64.)

Radical changes were in the offing for man when the Fall came. Up to that time our first parents were in the presence of God, their Father. Writing under the heading "Fall of Adam," Elder Bruce R. McConkie penned the following words which apply equally to both Adam and Eve:

> There was no death, no mortality, no corruption, no procrea-tion. . . .
>
> . . . He had temporal life because his spirit was housed in a temporal body, one made from the dust of the earth. (Abra. 5:7.) He had spiritual life because he was in the presence of God and was alive to the things of righteousness or of the Spirit. He had not yet come to that state of mortal probation in which are found the testings and trials requisite to a possible inheritance of eternal life. As yet the full knowledge of good and evil had not been placed before him; and, what was tremendously important in the eternal scheme of things, he could have no children. . . .
>
> In conformity with the will of the Lord, *Adam fell both spiritu-ally and temporally.* Spiritual death entered the world, meaning that man was cast out of the presence of the Lord and died as pertain-ing to the things of the Spirit which are the things of righteous-

ness. Temporal death also entered the world, meaning that man and all created things became mortal, and blood became the life preserving element in the natural body. In this mortal condition it became possible for the body and the spirit to separate, a separation which by definition is the natural or temporal death. (Alma 42:6-12; D&C 29:40-42.)

In this state of mortality, subject to both spiritual and temporal death, man thus was in a position to be examined relative to his worthiness to inherit eternal life. He became subject to corruption, disease, and all the ills of the flesh. Spiritually he was required to walk by faith rather than by sight; a knowledge of good and evil could now come to him by actual experience; and being mortal he could now have children, thus providing bodies for the pre-existent hosts. "Adam fell that men might be." (2 Ne.2:19-25; Moses 5:11; 6:45-48; *Doctrines of Salvation*, vol. 1, pp. 107-120.) [Bruce R. McConkie, *Mormon Doctrine*, pages 268-69].

We all understood and were taught this plan in the world of spirits before our world was formed. Thus, Peter talks of the redeeming Christ "who verily was foreordained before the foundation of the world, but was manifest in these last times for you." (1 Peter 1:20.) The time will come when we will be informed all about the manner of creation and the truths about the Fall. The Lord has promised that when he comes he will make all these things known. "Yea, verily I say unto you, in that day when the Lord shall come, he shall reveal all things — things which have passed, and hidden things which no man knew, things of the earth, by which it was made, and the purpose and the end therefore." (D&C 101:32-33.) Until that time we walk with scant knowledge. It is a matter of faith.

President Joseph Fielding Smith taught: "The fall of man came as a blessing in disguise, and was the means of furthering the purposes of the Lord in the progress of man, rather than a means of hindering them." (Joseph Fielding Smith, *Doctrines of Salvation*, 1:114.) Adam and Eve rejoiced in the fall. Adam said: "Blessed be the name of God, for because of my transgression my eyes are opened, and in this life I shall have joy, and again in the flesh I shall see God." And Eve added, "Were it not for our transgression we never should have had seed, and never should have known good and evil, and the joy of our redemption, and the eternal life which God giveth unto all the obedient." (Moses 5:10-11.)

In the economy of God, mortality was a necessary blessing that would be a harsh experience to the probationers. Clothed with mortal bodies men and women were to be subject to death, corruption, and all of the ills of the flesh. There were no promises that it would be easy. In the fallen state men and women are subject to the lusts, passions, and appetites of the flesh. They are in a "carnal state." (See Alma 41:10-11.) "Ye are yet carnal," Paul said to the Corinthian Saints, "for whereas there is among you envying, and strife, and divisions, are ye not carnal, and walk as men?" (1 Corinthians 3:3; see also Mosiah 3:19, and Bruce R. McConkie, *Mormon Doctrine,* page 113.)

The consequences of the Fall were partially enunciated to Eve by God. "Unto the woman he said, I will greatly multiply thy sorrow and thy conception; in sorrow thou shalt bring forth children; and thy desire shall be to thy husband, and he shall rule over thee." (Genesis 3:16.)

To bring us under a perfect law wherein husbands and wives deal intimately, tenderly, justly, and compassionately one with another, Paul instructs the Saints: "Husbands, love your wives, even as Christ also loved the church . . . so ought men to love their wives as their own bodies. He that loveth his wife loveth himself." (Ephesians 5:25, 28.)

Those who hold the priesthood are bound by principles of righteousness, as explained in the Doctrine and Covenants, section 121. Thus the only righteous influence a priesthood bearer has with his wife is exercised "by persuasion, by long-suffering, by gentleness and meekness, and by love unfeigned; by kindness, and pure knowledge. . . ." (D&C 121:41-42.) We may conclude that when a priesthood-bearing husband attempts at home "to exercise control or dominion or compulsion . . . in any degree of unrighteousness, behold, the heavens withdraw themselves; the Spirit of the Lord is grieved. . . ." (D&C 121:37.)

Men and women are of equal importance in the sight of God, who is no respecter of persons. There is no religious justification for unequal treatment of either sex. And as we have seen, in God's kingdom on earth it is expressly contrary to the revealed word for man to attempt to exercise dominion over women by compulsory means. Certainly this probationary estate is hard enough without one person trying to exercise unrighteous dominion over another. And since God is just, impartial, and kind, and since we are here on earth to be "added upon" not only physically but spiritually, we mortals would do well to emulate these attributes of the Father in heaven to whom we must one day give an accounting.

3

As God Views Woman

Like man, woman was created in the image of God. "So God created man in his own image, in the image of God created he him; male and female created he them." (Genesis 1:27.) The creation of persons in God's own image was the climax of the creative process. "And God saw everything that he had made, and, behold, it was very good." (Genesis 1:31.) When something is very good to God, it is indeed *very good*. That is how God viewed the newly created woman — very good.

How God views woman can be partially seen by a brief examination of her agency, her position before and after the Restoration, and her potential through celestial marriage.

Agency is an eternal principle. God gave man and woman the ability to choose, which he calls agency. The Lord said, "Behold I gave unto them their knowledge, in the day I created them; and in the Garden of Eden, gave I unto man his agency." (Moses 7:32.)

Agency is so fundamental a part of the great plan of creation and redemption that if it should cease, all other things would vanish away. "All truth is *independent* in that sphere in which God had placed it, *to act for itself*, as all intelligence also; *otherwise there is no existence.*" (D&C 93:30.) Expanding and interpreting this revealed principle, Lehi said: *"It must needs be, that there is an oppo-*

*sition in all things. If not so, . . . righteousness could not be brought to
pass, neither wickedness, neither holiness nor misery, neither good nor
bad."* [2 Nephi 2:11.] . . .

Agency is the philosophy of opposites. (Bruce R. McConkie,
Mormon Doctrine, pages 26-27.)

Opposites exist. Men and women may use their ability to choose.
In utilizing their agency men and women reap happiness and eternal
life, or misery and damnation, or some state in between. Without
agency there could be no judgment.

Satan "sought to destroy the agency of man." (Moses 4:3.) His
plan on earth is premised on compulsion. History is a sad story of
Satan's success. Men and women have been everywhere in chains.

"On the other hand, it is the will of the Lord that all [society should
be so structured]. 'That every man may act in doctrine and principle
pertaining to futurity, according to the moral agency which I have
given unto him, *that every man may be accountable for his own sins in the
day of judgment.'* (D&C 101:78.)" (Bruce R. McConkie, *Mormon Doctrine*,
pages 27-28.)

Free institutions have the approbation of God. Of the United
States God says, "I have established the Constitution of this land, by
the hands of wise men whom I raised up. . . ." (D&C 101:80.)

Status of Women

During this probationary estate women's lot in general has been
especially hard. Historically their role has often been made harder by
men who imposed "unrighteous dominion" by a wrong use of agency.
As the Lord whispered to the Prophet concerning the priesthood: "We
have learned by sad experience that it is the nature and disposition of
almost all men, as soon as they get a little authority, as they suppose,
they will immediately begin to exercise unrighteous dominion." (D&C
121:39.)

At the time of the restoration of the gospel the status of women
throughout the world was limited legally, socially, and economically.
It was a day of apostasy from the truth, including the truth about the
worth of women. There was limited light in the world. It is the fulness
of the gospel that brings clearly into focus the worth of each soul in the
eyes of God. Since the Restoration, attitudes have been reformed.

In the first half of the nineteenth century, women had little recognition as individuals in a legal sense. The early basic law of all states in
the United States, except Louisiana, had its origin in the English

common law, which in turn combined feudal and Roman laws. Common law is based on customs and ancient precedent. To state it at greater length, it comprises

the body of those principles and rules of action... which derive their authority solely from usages and customs of immemorial antiquities, or from the judgments and decrees of the courts recognizing, affirming, and enforcing such usages and customs, and in this sense particularly the ancient unwritten law of England. (1 *Kent Commentaries* 492.)

In the United States, common law is that body of rules and principles which were established and determined in England at the time the various states adopted it. Many of its principles have been changed by the Constitution and by statute.

An unmarried woman at common law had the capacity to contract and perform other legal acts on terms equal to that of a man. When she married, her position as a separate competent individual disappeared, and she was reduced to the legal capacity of a slave or an infant. The entire legal existence of a wife merged into that of her husband.

In her own capacity, a married woman could not validly sign a contract, deed, note or check; acquire or dispose of property without the consent of her husband; or sue or be sued. All personal property of the wife, whether acquired before or during the marriage, became that of her husband.

Upon the death of a husband his property (including that acquired from his wife) generally went to his estate. The wife was permitted to keep her "paraphernalia," which included wearing apparel and jewelry she was wearing. Even these, except for the clothing required by modesty, could be taken to satisfy her husband's debts.

Similarly harsh rules applied to real property. That acquired prior to her marriage became subject to her husband's wishes. He could sell or mortgage without her consent. He was entitled to the rent from crops and had no duty to account to her for money received.

If a wife were employed to act as a midwife, as a seamstress, or in any other capacity, her husband was entitled to her pay.

A New Hampshire judge in 1830 described the inability of a wife to make a will by saying she was "considered to be so entirely under the power of the husband, that she could, in no case, make what in propriety of speech is called a Will." (*Marston v. Norton,* Superior Court of New Hampshire, 5 N.H. 205.)

A mother's right to her children was inferior to that of her husband, as illustrated by a decision of the New York Supreme Court in

1842. "The question then is, which of these parents, the father or the mother, has the best title to the custody of the child? The opinion of the court has been repeatedly expressed, that by the law of the land the claims of the father are superior to those of the mother." (*Mercein v. The People* ex rel. Barry, 3 Hill [N.Y.] 399.)

Until recent years, a woman who had citizenship status before her marriage lost it upon marriage to an alien. Also, the franchise, the right to vote, did not come to most women until the twentieth century.

These were the common legal situations in the United States prior to the time when the gospel was restored.

Twelve years after the Church was organized the Prophet Joseph Smith made this comment in inaugurating the women's organization of the Church: "And now I turn the key in your behalf in the name of the Lord, and this Society [the female Relief Society] shall rejoice, and knowledge and intelligence shall flow down from this time henceforth." (Joseph Smith, *History of the Church,* 4:607.) That was in 1842.

While this remark was made in the context of charitable works and priesthood direction for the members of the new society, it is interesting to observe, from our vantage point in history, that knowledge and intelligence indeed increased in the United States generally, as in other lands. From about the time "the key was turned," woman's position has bettered in innumerable ways. With apostasy had come derogation to womankind. With Restoration came women's rights and privileges. Scores of years before the twentieth-century right to vote was conferred upon women, President Brigham Young was encouraging women. "Now, sisters, I want you to vote also, because women are the characters that rule the ballot box." (*Discourses of Brigham Young,* ed. John A. Widtsoe [Deseret Book Co., 1954], page 367.)

The result of all this is that in many respects married women of today enjoy rights superior to those of married men. For instance, in many states a married woman is vested with a right to one-third of all the real property owned by her husband during the marriage. The husband does not have a corresponding interest in his wife's real property. In these same states a wife can convey her property without her husband's consent, but the husband must have his wife's approval before he can convey property. Also, many states now give women, by statute, a preferential right to the custody of the children in divorce cases.

All this change to woman's advantage has taken place since the restoration of the gospel. The spirit of that gospel has helped to bring fulfillment to womankind in the here and now.

Celestial Marriage

God has made known his view on marriage. In the second chapter of the Bible he is quoted as saying, "It is not good that man should be alone." (Genesis 2:18.) "Therefore shall a man leave his father and his mother, and shall cleave unto his wife: and they shall be one flesh." (Genesis 2:24.) The first chapter of the Bible tells of creation itself. The very next item of business in God's priority of things is marriage. The most prominent of Christian missionaries in the apostolic age, the apostle Paul, sums up the matter of marriage in the wholeness of life by saying, "Neither is the man without the woman, neither the woman without the man, in the Lord." (1 Corinthians 11:11.) Thus, marriage is ordained of God. It is part of his law and order of things.

The law of Christ is a celestial law. It is the law by obedience to which men and women gain an inheritance in the glory of the celestial kingdom in eternity. "And they who are not sanctified through the law which I have given unto you, even the law of Christ, must inherit another kingdom, . . . for he who is not able to abide the law of a celestial kingdom cannot abide a celestial glory." (D&C 88:21-22.)

If men and women obey the celestial law in this life, they gain celestial bodies and celestial spirits — that is, in the resurrection they receive their bodies back again quickened with celestial glory. Thus they become qualified to enter into the celestial kingdom of God. (See D&C 88:16-20, 28-29; 1 Corinthians 15:40-42.) The term *salvation* nearly always means to be saved in the celestial kingdom.

However, not all persons in the celestial kingdom go on to exaltation. "In the celestial glory there are three heavens or degrees." (D&C 131:1.) Some persons, even in the celestial kingdom, are "without exaltation, in their saved condition, to all eternity." (D&C 132:17.) Such will be "ministering servants, to minister for those who are worthy of a far more, and an exceeding, and an eternal weight of glory." (D&C 132:16.) "There is no gift greater than the gift of salvation." (D&C 6:13.) Full and complete salvation consists of eternal life, the kind and type and quality of life that God himself enjoys.

Celestial marriage is God's form and type of marriage. He instituted it. We have seen that he performed the first such marriage. Marriages performed under his sanction, in his temples and by virtue of his sealing power, are called celestial marriages. They are marriages obedient to celestial law. "The participating parties become husband and wife in this mortal life, and if after their marriage [ceremony] they keep all the terms and conditions of the order of the priesthood, they continue on as husband and wife in the celestial kingdom of God."

(Bruce R. McConkie, *Mormon Doctrine,* page 117.) All other marriages or contracts and obligations of every kind that are not "sealed by the Holy Spirit of promise . . . for time and for all eternity . . . are of no efficacy, virtue, or force in and after the resurrection from the dead; for all contracts that are not made unto this end have an end when men are dead." (D&C 132:7.) Celestial marriage is an ordinance of exaltation. Those who do not enter into this ordinance and covenant do not receive the blessings conditioned upon obedience to the law that requires it.

This marriage is called "the new and everlasting covenant of marriage." (D&C 131:2.) It is new in that it has been revealed anew in this generation; and it is everlasting because it has been forever in the past and will be forever in the future.

> For behold, I reveal unto you a new and everlasting covenant; . . .
>
> For all who will have a blessing at my hands shall abide the law which was appointed for that blessing, and the conditions thereof, as were instituted from before the foundation of the world.
>
> And as pertaining to the new and everlasting covenant, it was instituted for the fulness of my glory; and he that receiveth a fulness thereof must and shall abide the law. (D&C 132:4-6.)

God's quality of life is, in a measure, dependent upon his type and quality of marriage — celestial marriage.

> Therefore, if a man marry him a wife in the world, and he marry her not by me nor by my word, and he covenant with her so long as he is in the world and she with him, their covenant and marriage are not of force when they are dead, and when they are out of the world; therefore, they are not bound by any law when they are out of the world.
>
> Therefore, when they are out of the world they neither marry nor are given in marriage; but are appointed angels in heaven, which angels are ministering servants, to minister for those who are worthy of a far more, and an exceeding, and an eternal weight of glory.
>
> For these angels did not abide my law; therefore, they cannot be enlarged, but remain separately and singly, without exaltation, in their saved condition, to all eternity; and from henceforth are not gods, but are angels of God forever and ever. (D&C 132:15-17.)

As celestial marriage is a covenant of exaltation, its ultimate fruit is the gaining of exaltation. Through the practice of this principle and ordinance men and women may have eternal increase, "a continuation of the seeds forever and ever," a continuation of lives, and eternal lives. (D&C 132:19.) That is, they may procreate spirit children after the resurrection and may, in due course, inherit all that our Father has. (See D&C 76:60-70; 93:1-20.)

All blessings are predicated upon obedience to law. With reference to God's marriage law, he says, "Verily, verily, I say unto you, except ye abide my law ye cannot attain to this glory.... But if ye receive me in the world, then shall ye know me, and shall receive your exaltation; that where I am ye shall be also." (D&C 132:21-23.) The gospel helps to fulfill womankind in the ultimate scheme of things.

God has spoken clearly with reference to the sanctity and necessity of marriage. Divine fiat thunders from the heavens: "Receive ye, therefore, my law." (D&C 132:24.)

All men and women are children of God. He has declared it his purpose to bring about the fulfillment of his children in every way. "For behold, this is my work and my glory — to bring to pass the immortality and eternal life of man." (Moses 1:39.) In accomplishing this purpose "God is no respecter of persons." (Acts 10:34.) Man and woman alike, he offers us all the same ultimate rewards.

4

Exemplary Women of the Bible

Bone of my bones, and flesh of my flesh: she shall be called Woman," Adam said. (Genesis 2:23.) In her creation woman was the helpmeet of man. (See Genesis 2:18, 21-24.) In early times women labored in the fields and took care of sheep. (See Genesis 29:9; Exodus 2:16; Ruth 2:3,8.) However, their main duties consisted of household and family tasks such as grinding grain (Matthew 24:41), caring for the physical needs of the family (1 Samuel 2:19; 2 Samuel 13:8; Acts 9:36-39), supervising the home (1 Timothy 5:14), and instructing the children. (See Proverbs 1:8, 31:1; Titus 2:4-5.) Under the Mosaic law the wife and the mother were to be respected and honored. (See Exodus 20:12; Proverbs 18:22; Ecclesiastes 9:9.)

While less than one hundred women are cited by name in the Bible, many others are mentioned in terms of the deeds and roles they performed. Women served in a variety of occupations; their talents extended beyond the home.

Mothers are particularly praised. Reverence for mothers is a repeated theme. (See 1 Kings 2:19, 20; Proverbs 23:22.) One of the Ten Commandments, the first one with a promise, thundered from the heavens, "Honour thy father and thy mother: that thy days may be long upon the land which the Lord thy God giveth thee." (Exodus 20:12.) Children are to be obedient to their mothers. (See Proverbs 1:8.)

Mother's prayers are answered. (See 1 Samuel 1:27.) Their teachings are virtuous. (See Proverbs 31:1-31.)

Starting with the mother of all living, Eve, there are many famous biblical mothers: Deborah, "a mother in Israel" (see Judges 5:7); Sarah, "mother of nations" (see Genesis 17:15,16); Hannah, mother of the prophet Samuel (see 1 Samuel 1-28); Bathsheba, mother of Solomon (see 2 Samuel 11:24); Mary, the mother of Christ (see Luke 2:5-11).

Prophetesses, women divinely called to prophesy, are also found in Bible history. Such were Miriam (see Exodus 15:20-21; Numbers 12:2; Micah 6:4), Deborah (see Judges 4:4-6, 14), Huldah (see 2 Kings 22:14-20), and the daughters of Philip, the evangelist (see Acts 21:8-9).

Queens, the wives of kings or women reigning in their own right, were given special attention in the Bible. Biblical queens include: Athaliah (see 2 Kings 11:1,3); Candace, of Ethiopia (see Acts 8:27); Esther, favorite wife of King Ahasuerus (see Esther 2:15-17); Jezebel, wife of Ahab, king of Israel, and power behind the throne (see 1 Kings 16:30-31); Queen of Sheba, propounder of riddles to Solomon (see 1 Kings 10:1-13); Tahpenes, Queen of Egypt (see 1 Kings 11:19).

Lydia, who sold dyed garments, was singled out for special mention in the New Testament. (See Acts 16:14-15.)

Wives also are mentioned specifically. Some of their duties, and the duties of their husbands to them, are set forth in the New Testament. (See Ephesians 5:22-29; Titus 2:4-5; 1 Peter 3:1-7.)

From the occupations and roles mentioned, we can see that recorded history does indeed witness that women labored alongside of men. (See Moses 5:1.) It has always been intended that women be productive, contributing, fulfilled human beings. With her husband, woman was given dominion over the earth.

One of today's greatest needs is for worthy models. Let us examine some of the superlative women of the Bible who can be such models.

Eve

Eve "was the mother of all living" (Genesis 3:20) and is one to whom we all look for our beginning on earth. As "the mother of all living" she deserves the honor we are told to give to our parents. (See Exodus 20:12.) Notwithstanding this, there is little knowledge available to us about Eve.

Eve's husband, as one of the spirit sons of God, was unequaled in pre-earth existence by anyone except the Firstborn Christ himself. None of the billions of our Father's children who were to live on this earth attained Adam's stature and power and intelligence and might there, save Jesus only. It is assumed that he sat in the council of the gods when the creation of the earth was planned, and then, under Christ, participated in the creative process. (See Abraham 3:22-26.) He was Michael the archangel. (See Oscar W. McConkie, Jr., *Angels* [Deseret Book Co., 1975], pages 42-44.)

Unfortunately, we are not told of Eve's achievements before this earth life. However, there is no question in my mind but that she was equally a special spirit, just as Adam was. Since she was chosen to become the first woman here on earth, her diligence and obedience in her first estate must have brought her to a stature like that of the one chosen to be the first man. In intelligence and devotion to righteousness Eve and Adam were compatible spirits. Their mission required two such individuals.

"She [Eve] was placed on earth in the same manner as was Adam, the Mosaic account of the Lord creating her from Adam's rib being merely figurative." (Bruce R. McConkie, *Mormon Doctrine,* page 242.)

When Eve was placed on the earth, the earth was in a paradisiacal glory. Death had not yet come into the world. In this Edenic condition she was married to Adam in the new and everlasting covenant of celestial marriage, the ceremony being performed by God himself. Theirs was an eternal covenant and union.

Eve partook of the "forbidden fruit." (The real meaning of the expression "forbidden fruit" has not been revealed.) She and then Adam disobeyed God's directive to not eat of the tree of the knowledge of good and evil. Their disobedience to this command brought death, or in other words mortality, into the world. (See Moses 3:17.)

In all of this Eve and Adam simply "complied with the law which enabled them to become mortal beings, and this course of conduct is termed eating the forbidden fruit." (Bruce R. McConkie, *Mormon Doctrine,* page 289.) This is the way their bodies were changed from immortal to mortal, physical bodies that would be capable of having children. Eve partook of the forbidden fruit first. "Adam was not deceived, but the woman being deceived was in the transgression." (1 Timothy 2:14.) That is, after Eve partook, Adam partook in order for them to remain together and to comply with the command to multiply and to fill the earth with posterity.

While we do not know the real meaning of the term *forbidden fruit,* we do know that it was not sexual intercourse. It is an apostate tradition contrary to the scriptures to suppose that our first parents entered into immoral sexual indulgence and that this action constituted forbidden fruit. Eve and Adam were married before Eve partook of the forbidden fruit, and God had commanded them to have children. (Moses 2:28.)

After the Fall, after man and woman became mortal, the Lord said to Eve, "I will greatly multiply thy sorrow and thy conception. In sorrow thou shalt bring forth child, and thy desire shall be to thy husband, and he shall rule over thee." (Moses 4:22.)

We are left to assume that Eve was like Michael in the pre-earth existence. We are given evidence that she was as intelligent and right-minded as her husband in this second estate of existence. One of the most perfect summaries of the plan of salvation ever given fell from the lips of Eve. As Adam was filled with the Spirit and taught the gospel, Eve responded:

> And Eve, his wife, heard all these things and was glad, saying: Were it not for our transgression we never should have seed, and never should have known good and evil, and the joy of our redemption, and the eternal life which God giveth unto all the obedient.
>
> And Adam and Eve blessed the name of God, and they made all things known unto their sons and daughters. (Moses 5:11-12.)

How was Eve taught so that she could give such a perfect account? After the Fall, Eve and Adam were cast out of the Garden of Eden. They "called upon the name of the Lord, and they heard the voice of the Lord.... And he gave unto them commandments, that they should worship the Lord their God." (Moses 5:4-5.)

Note that both Eve and Adam prayed. They both heard the voice of the Lord. Both of them were commanded to worship and serve their creator.

We can see from these citations that Eve was a joint participant with Adam in his ministry. She was an active participant. She will inherit jointly with him.

Adam and Eve, the great prototype of man and woman — of husband and wife, of mother and father — were equal in quality.

Sarah

Sarah was the wife of father Abraham. She was also his niece, the daughter of his brother Haran (Abraham 2:2), although he once referred to her as "the daughter of my father, but not the daughter of my mother" (Genesis 20:12). She was ten years younger than Abraham and lived for 127 years. She came with her husband from Ur of Chaldees. (See Genesis 11:28-31, 17:17.) Sarah's name was changed from Sarai to Sarah at the time she was promised a child, when she was ninety. (See Genesis 17:15-16.) Though there are several exemplary episodes in the life of Sarah, we shall consider her central mission in life as our model.

Sarah and her husband first received the gospel by baptism. This is the covenant of salvation. They then entered into celestial marriage. This is the covenant of exaltation. Properly observed and implemented, this covenant assures eternal increase. Finally, they received the promise that all of these blessings would be offered to their mortal posterity. (See Abraham 2:6-11; D&C 132:29-39, 49.) Included in the divine promises to Abraham and Sarah was the assurance that Christ would come through their lineage and that their posterity would receive certain promised lands as an inheritance. (See Abraham 2:6, 9-11, 18; Genesis 17:4-8, 15-16, 19-21; 22:15-18; Galatians 3:6-29.) All of these covenants taken together are called the Abrahamic covenant. It is clear that Sarah and Abraham were full partners in this joint venture.

The Lord said to Abraham, "I will make thy seed as the dust of the earth: so that if a man can number the dust of the earth, then shall thy seed also be numbered." (Genesis 13:16.) One of Sarah's most noble unselfish moments is recorded as she was attempting to fulfill this promise. "And Sarai said unto Abram, Behold now, the Lord hath restrained me from bearing: I pray thee, go in unto my maid; it may be that I may obtain children by her." (Genesis 16:2.)

After a life of testing, Sarah was promised a son of her own. The promise came after Sarah had passed her childbearing years. "Now Abraham and Sarah were old and well stricken in age; and it ceased to be with Sarah after the manner of women. Therefore Sarah laughed within herself, saying, After I am waxed old shall I have pleasure, my lord being old also?" (Genesis 18:11-12.) But nothing was too hard for the Lord. And Sarah conceived and bore a son according to the word of the Lord. At the time of the birth she was ninety years old. Her mission was to "be a mother of nations." (Genesis 17:16.)

It was again pertaining to her central role of producing a chosen people that the heavens were opened and God spoke to her husband again. "And God said unto Abraham, . . . all that Sarah hath said unto thee, hearken unto her voice." (Genesis 21:12.) LDS wives and mothers would feel greatly blessed to have that kind of divine approbation.

The Abrahamic covenant was renewed with Isaac (see Genesis 24:60; 26:1-4) and again with Jacob (Genesis 28:1-5, 10-14; 35:9-13; 48:3-4). Those portions of it which have to do with personal exaltation and eternal increase are renewed with each member of the house of

Israel who enters the order of celestial marriage. Through that order of marriage, participants become inheritors of all of the blessings of Abraham, Isaac, and Jacob. (See D&C 132; Romans 9:4; Galatians 3:6-9.)

"We be Abraham's seed," the Jews said. (John 8:33.) And so they were in a literal sense. But in the gospel sense Abraham and Sarah's children are those who do the works of Abraham and Sarah. They are adopted into that lineage. (See Abraham 2:8-11; D&C 84:33-34; 132:29-33.) Hence, our Lord replied to the Jews, "If ye were Abraham's children, ye would do the works of Abraham." (John 8:39.)

The author has elsewhere written:

> The Elias of Abraham's day came to Joseph Smith. . . . What did this Elias give to the earth again? The gospel of Abraham. And what is the gospel of Abraham? What is that portion of the good news of salvation particularly associated with Abraham? It is a divine promise that his seed should continue 'as innumerable as the stars; or, if ye were to count the sand upon the seashore ye could not number them.' . . . This promise is to apply out of this world as well as in this world. The gospel especially associated with Abraham was the gospel of celestial marriage. . . . It is the commission to provide a lineage for the elect portion of the pre-earth spirits of the Eternal Father. It is a gospel to provide a mansion in heaven for those who lived the celestial law here. This is what was restored. As a result of this portion of the restoration, the righteous among future generations were assured the continuation of seeds forever, even as it was with Abraham of old. (Oscar W. McConkie, *Angels*, page 55.)

Mothers in Israel and daughters of Zion, look to Sarah as your exemplar. Join in the Abrahamic covenant of celestial marriage: "And I will bless them that bless thee, . . . and in thee shall all families of the earth be blessed." (Genesis 12:3.)

Rebekah

Another common ancestor, Rebekah, shows her daughters in the world today what they can do. The glimpses we are given of her life should be a pattern.

First, Rebekah was a virgin until she was selected as a wife for Isaac. "Rebekah came out. . . . And the damsel was very fair to look upon, a virgin, neither had any man known her." (Genesis 24:15-16.) Apparently, this was one of the prerequisites for her selection. The reward for her modesty and other qualities was a God-provided husband of strength, means, and righteousness.

Second, she was responsive to parental guidance. "Behold, Rebekah is before thee, take her, and go, and let her be thy master's son's wife, as the Lord has spoken." (Genesis 24:51.) Mature parents, schooled in listening to the whispering of the Spirit, are a valuable aid to young adults during courtship and selection of spouses. Parents are resources that daughters of Zion should use. Shared judgment and wisdom is helpful in selecting an eternal companion.

Third, despite her supplications to the Lord, Rebekah was barren. "And Isaac intreated the Lord for his wife, because she was barren, and the Lord was intreated of him, and Rebekah his wife conceived." (Genesis 25:21.) This is a perfect example of a proper partnership in marriage. The husband goes to the Lord and asks him for the special blessings that are the desires of the wife's heart (and in this case of the husband's heart also). We should not suppose that if Rebekah had not been supportive of Isaac in his ministry, if she had not helped him use properly his God-given powers of intercession, she would have been the beneficiary of his petitioning God in her behalf.

Fourth, and here is the great example that Rebekah puts before us, she inquired of the Lord when something seemed amiss. Jacob and Esau while yet in the womb struggled together. Rebekah was troubled. "Why am I thus?" she asked. She needed divine guidance, so she took the matter up with the Lord and he spoke to her in reply. The scripture says: "And she went to inquire of the Lord. And the Lord said unto her, Two nations are in thy womb," and then he described them. (Genesis 25:22-23.) Rebekah knew that the Lord gives revelation as needed to women who pray to him in faith.

Finally, when Jacob and Esau had grown to maturity the greatest concern of their parents was the matter of whom they should marry. The record says that Esau "took to wife Judith the daughter of Beeri the Hittite, and Bashemath the daughter of Elon the Hittite: which were a grief of mind unto Isaac and to Rebekah." (Genesis 26:34-35.) Esau had married out of the faith; he did not enter the Lord's system of celestial marriage, and his marriage brought great sorrow to his parents.

Rebekah had great anxiety as to whom Jacob would marry. She was fearful that he too might depart from the teachings of his parents and marry someone who was not eligible to receive the blessing of eternal marriage. The scripture says, "And Rebekah said to Isaac, I am weary of my life because of the daughters of Heth: if Jacob takes a wife of the daughters of Heth, such as these which are of the daughters of the land, what good shall my life do me?" (Genesis 27:46.)

That is to say, Rebekah thought her whole life would be wasted if Jacob too married out of the Church. She knew he could not enter the gate leading to exaltation unless he was married in the new and everlasting covenant of marriage, so she brought the matter to Isaac's attention.

This is a great object lesson. The mother was greatly concerned about the marriage of her son, and she prevailed upon the father to do something about it. Rebekah was acting as a guide and a light to Jacob (as my wife often does to me).

It seems very clear to me that Rebekah said to her husband, in effect, "You must see that Jacob marries one of my relatives, one who is faithful to the Lord. We can't afford to take a chance."

The account goes on: "And Isaac called Jacob, and blessed him, and charged him, and said unto him, Thou shalt not take a wife of the daughters of Canaan." (Genesis 28:1.)

How many members of the Church have received patriarchal blessings in which they were told to marry in the temple for time and eternity? So it was with Jacob. Isaac gave him a blessing that meant: Don't marry out of the Church.

The blessing continued, "Arise, go to Padanaram, to the house of Bethuel thy mother's father; and take a wife from thence of the daughters of Laban thy mother's brother. And God Almighty bless thee, and make thee fruitful, . . . And give thee the blessing of Abraham." (Genesis 28:2-4.)

The scriptural account suggests that Rebekah manned the laboring oar in all of this. It certainly appears that Rebekah's greatness was equal to her husband's.

"And Jacob Loved Rachel"

There is yet another woman whose destiny was to assist her husband in his incomparable promise, "And thy seed shall be as the dust of the earth, and thou shalt spread abroad . . . and in thee and in thy seed shall all the families of the earth be blessed." (Genesis 28:14.) The husband was Jacob, son of Isaac and Rebekah, whose name was later changed to Israel. (See Genesis 32:28.)

It was the mighty Moses who said: "When the most High divided to the nations their inheritance, when he separated the sons of Adam, he set the bounds of the people according to the number of the children of Israel." (Deuteronomy 32:8.) That is to say, many of the noble and great spirits from pre-earth life were to be assigned to come through the blood lineage of Israel. This "believing blood" was to be a blessing to all the inhabitants of the world. Would one suppose that the mothers of Israel's children played the central and lead roles in this drama?

Jacob did as his mother, the Lord, and his father bade him to do. He traveled to Padanaram for the express purpose of marrying one of his Uncle Laban's daughters. He first saw his cousin Rachel as she worked. After arriving in the strange land he inquired about Laban, and Rachel was pointed out: "His daughter cometh with the sheep. . . . Rachel came with her father's sheep: for she kept them." (Genesis 29: 6, 9.)

This meeting was an emotional experience. We could call it love at first sight. "And Jacob kissed Rachel, and lifted up his voice, and wept. . . . Rachel was beautiful and well favoured. And Jacob loved Rachel." (Genesis 29:11, 17-18.)

Jacob agreed to serve Laban seven years if Laban would give him his daughter Rachel for a wife. After he had served for the seven years, Laban cheated him by giving him instead Rachel's older sister, Leah, for a wife. By agreement, Jacob then lived with Leah for a week, at the end of which time Laban gave him Rachel as his second wife; and Jacob further agreed to serve another seven years to complete his service to Laban for the two wives.

Jacob also took Leah's and Rachel's two handmaids Zilpah and Bilhah to wife. During the twenty years Jacob stayed with Laban, Leah and the handmaids bore him ten sons and one daughter, and Rachel bore him one son, Joseph. While they traveled in the land of promise, Rachel died giving Israel another son, Benjamin.

Israel spoke of his issue as "the children which God hath graciously given thy servant." (Genesis 33:5.) The theme of the patriarchs was always to this effect: "Lo, children are an heritage of the Lord: and the fruit of the womb is his reward." (Psalm 127:3.) "And God remembered Rachel, and God hearkened to her, and opened her womb. And she conceived, and bare a son; and said, God hath taken away my reproach." (Genesis 30:22-23.)

God listened to Rachel's prayers, and she was granted the righteous desire of her heart — she bore children. In this she has been a righteous model for wives in all generations after her.

What kind of a wife was this superior woman? Under the most difficult of circumstances, those of choosing her husband over her father and all she held dear, she was first a wife. Leah was one with Rachel in sustaining their husband. They said to him, "Whatsoever God hath said unto thee, do." (Genesis 31:16.) With the example of the sustaining influence of such wives "Jacob rose up," with his family and goods, "to go to Isaac his father in the land of Canaan." (Genesis 31:17-18.)

Rachel died in Canaan. In the generations to come the elders of Israel reverently praised her name, using her and Leah as a standard: "The Lord make the woman that is come into thine house like Rachel and like Leah, which two did build the house of Israel: and do thou worthily." (Ruth 4:11.)

It appears that the members of the husband-wife teams Eve and Adam, Sarah and Abraham, Rebekah and Isaac, and Rachel and Leah and Jacob — or Israel — were equally yoked in the service of God and his purposes on the earth.

A Great Widow

While examining model women from the Bible, we should consider an example that demonstrates the way in which the blessings of heaven may be obtained.

It happened in Zarephath, a town of Phoenicia near Sidon. The characters in the incident reported are Elijah, one of the greatest of the prophets, an unnamed widow, her son, and the God of heaven.

Elijah appeared suddenly during the reign of Ahab, a wicked king of Israel (about 873-851 B.C.) to denounce the king and his wife, Jezebel, for their idolatry and crimes. His purpose was to save Israel from the worship of Baal. He was God's agent in bringing about a drought in retribution against the people because of their wickedness. "And Elijah . . . said unto Ahab, As the Lord God of Israel liveth, before whom I stand, there shall not be dew nor rain these years, but according to my word." (1 Kings 17:1.) With the heavens shut up and rain nonexistent, the brooks dried up. (See 1 Kings 17:7.) Such righteous persons as there were suffered with the wicked.

The Lord directed his prophet to go to a widow in Zarephath for sustenance.

> And when he came to the gate of the city, behold, the widow woman was there gathering of sticks: and he called to her, and said, Fetch me, I pray thee, a little water in a vessel, that I may drink.
>
> And as she was going to fetch it, he called to her, and said, Bring me, I pray thee, a morsel of bread in thine hand.
>
> And she said, As the Lord thy God liveth, I have not a cake, but an handful of meal in a barrel, and a little oil in a cruse: and, behold, I am gathering two sticks, that I may go in and dress it for me and my son, that we may eat it, and die.
>
> And Elijah said unto her, Fear not; go and do as thou hast said: but make me thereof a little cake first, and bring it unto me, and after make for thee and for thy son.

For thus saith the Lord God of Israel, The barrel of meal shall not waste, neither shall the cruse of oil fail, until the day that the Lord sendeth rain upon the earth.

And she went and did according to the saying of Elijah: and she, and he, and her house, did eat many days.

And the barrel of meal wasted not, neither did the cruse of oil fail, according to the word of the Lord, which he spake by Elijah. (1 Kings 17:10-16.)

Beautiful, a perfect example! The Lord seemed to be requiring so much. He asked for all that the widow had, her very necessities of life. The only promise in return was "fear not," that her needs would be taken care of. There seemed to be no natural way that the Lord's promise could be kept. This is the trial of faith. In large measure we walk by faith in this earth life. The woman obeyed God's messenger, and it was as he said: miraculously her food did not diminish. God cared for her needs. She and her son were sustained. They did not perish in the drought and resulting famine as they had supposed they would. The significant principle is that *the promised blessing followed the trial of faith*. This is the pattern.

God fulfilled his promise every whit. The woman was to care for the wants of his servant, and God would care for the wants of the woman and her son. It was done.

Then came the Lord's bonus. Subsequent to the foregoing incident the son of the woman fell sick, "and his sickness was so sore, that there was no breath left in him." (1 Kings 17:17.) The boy died. The grief-stricken mother bemoaned her loss to Elijah. Elijah "cried unto the Lord, and said, O Lord my God, . . . I pray thee, let this child's soul come into him again. And the Lord heard the voice of Elijah; and the soul of the child came into him again, and he revived." (1 Kings 17:20-22.) Elijah then took the child to his mother and said, "See, thy son liveth." (1 Kings 17:23.)

Whatever we are required to do by the Lord, no matter how difficult it may appear to us, if we keep the commandments we are blessed beyond our deserving. It is as King Benjamin told his people:

I say unto you that if ye should serve him who has created you from the beginning, and is preserving you from day to day, by lending you breath, that ye may live and move and do according to your own will, and even supporting you from one moment to another — I say, if ye should serve him with all your whole souls yet ye would be unprofitable servants.

And behold, all that he requires of you is to keep his commandments; and he has promised you that if ye would keep his

commandments ye should prosper in the land; and he never doth
vary from that which he hath said; therefore, if ye do keep his
commandments he doth bless you and prosper you.

And now, in the first place, he hath created you, and granted
unto you your lives, for which ye are indebted unto him.

And secondly, he doth require that ye should do as he hath
commanded you; for which if ye do, he doth immediately bless
you; and therefore he hath paid you. And ye are still indebted unto
him, and are, and will be, forever and ever; therefore, of what
have ye to boast? (Mosiah 2:21-24.)

The widow of Zarephath is the example before us as to how to get
the blessings of heaven. If we obey God he will open the window of
heaven and pour out blessings upon us.

Esther the Queen

The first recorded "beauty contest" took place about 485 B.C.
Ahasuerus was the reigning monarch from India to Ethiopia. He ruled
over 127 provinces. (See Esther 1:1.) He invited all the princes of Persia
and Media to a feast. His queen, Vashti, "made a feast for the women."
On the seventh day of the feast he commanded his servants "to bring
Vashti the queen before the king with the crown royal, to shew the
people and the princes her beauty: for she was fair to look on. But the
queen Vashti refused to come at the king's commandment." (Esther
1:11-12.)

This caused no small stir. The king inquired of his wise men to
know what to do to the queen. "For this deed of the queen shall come
abroad unto all women, so that they shall despise their husbands in
their eyes. . . . Thus shall there arise too much contempt and wrath."
(Esther 1:17-18.)

In the end it was determined that "the king give her royal estate
unto another that is better than she." (Esther 1:19.) The rationale was
that the disposition of the case would encourage "all the wives [to] give
to their husbands honour, both to great and small." It was public policy
"that every man should bear rule in his own house." (Esther 1:22.) And
so it was written, and so it was done, according to the law of the Medes
and Persians (which was far from being a perfect law).

Then came the business of selecting a new queen. And here we
have an Old Testament version of an international beauty contest. The
rules were set by the state. There is no evidence that entrance into the
contest was optional; "Officers in all the provinces of [the] kingdom"
were to gather "all the fair young virgins [to] the palace, . . . and let

the maiden which pleaseth the king be queen instead of Vashti."
(Esther 2:3-4.)

There was a Jew named Mordecai who was rearing an uncle's child
— Esther — as his own daughter, "for she had neither father nor
mother, and the maid was fair and beautiful." So later, when the king's
decree was heard, and when many young girls were brought to the
palace, Esther was also brought to the king's house.

"And the maiden pleased him, and she obtained kindness of
him: . . . and he preferred her. . . . The king delighted in her. . . . And
the king loved Esther above all the women, and she obtained grace and
favour in his sight more than all the virgins; so that he set the royal
crown upon her head, and made her queen instead of Vashti." (Esther
2:7, 9, 14, 17.) It appears that this romantic story served God's purposes.

Prince Haman was advanced by the king and was set above all
other princes. "And all the king's servants that were in the king's gate,
bowed, and reverenced Haman: for the king had so commanded
concerning him. But Mordecai bowed not, nor did him reverence. . . .
And when Haman saw that Mordecai bowed not, nor did him reverence, then was Haman full of wrath." (Esther 3:2, 5.) The result of
Haman's injured pride was an attempt to destroy the Jews. This is an
early example of attempted mass extermination. Haman convinced the
king that "a certain people . . . dispersed . . . in all the provinces" were
in rebellion, and in this way he got an extermination order against the
Jews.

Esther determined to make supplication to the king to save her
people. It took some planning for her to have access to the king. Under
the law no one could come to the king without being called. The king
had not called for Esther for thirty days.

Esther asked Mordecai to have the Jewish community join her in
fasting to the end that she could successfully approach her husband.
The strictness of the law of Persians and the Medes made this an even
more dramatic incident: "And fast ye for me, and neither eat nor drink
three days, night or day: I also and my maidens will fast likewise; and
so will I go in unto the king, which is not according to the law: and if I
perish, I perish." (Esther 4:16.) I find this a great example of courage.

At the conclusion of the fast Esther put on her best royal apparel
and stood in the inner court so the king could see her. The king held out
his golden sceptre as a sign that she could come to him. She invited the
king and Haman to a banquet she had prepared. The king was pleased
to accept her invitation.

The heavens intervened to prepare the king for the request his wife was planning to make at the banquet. The fasting and prayers had been answered. "And the king said again unto Esther on the second day at the banquet of wine, What is thy petition, queen Esther? and it shall be granted thee: and what is thy request? and it shall be performed, even to the half of the kingdom.

"Then Esther the queen answered and said, If I have found favour in thy sight, O king, and if it please the king, let my life be given me at my petition, and my people at my request: For we are sold, I and my people, to be destroyed, to be slain, and to perish." (Esther 7:2, 4.) The queen continued to petition her husband, saying that she could not endure to see her kindred destroyed, that it was a great evil.

The king's heart was softened, and he gave his wife the righteous desires of her heart. He even had Mordecai write the royal decree in words and terms of Mordecai's choice, and "the Jews had light, and gladness, and joy, and honour." (Esther 8:16.)

Wives ought to exercise this kind of influence upon their husbands. If the husband is the head, then the wife is the neck and constantly helps determine a proper course of action. This is what "an help meet" is. Abraham Lincoln is quoted as saying, "Behind every great man is a great woman." Queen Esther, the beautiful daughter of Abihail, a Benjamite, shows us the way in this exemplary attribute of womankind.

There is an equally important lesson inherent in this historical narrative. It is expressed by Mordecai: "Who knoweth whether thou art come to the kingdom for such a time as this?" (Esther 4:14.) Esther's providential position was according to the plan and purposes of God. This woman was an agent on God's errand. Others with special endowments with which they achieve prominence and influence would do well to use their positions of strength to make God's purposes their own.

We need to further focus on the fact that Esther understood that she had a higher allegiance than to her husband, and that was to her God. It was her sense of self-direction which was essential to her request to the Jewish people that they supplicate the Lord. Her sense of right prevailed and God gave his approbation to her act of courage.

Mary

Let us now consider the blessed virgin whom the Father chose to be the mother of his Son.

I believe the first sense of real empathy I felt for a scriptural character came when I was reading one of Nephi's superlative religious experiences. Some six hundred years before Christ, Nephi wanted to have the same experience that his father had enjoyed. Nephi records: "I had desired to know the things that my father had seen, and believing that the Lord was able to make them known unto me, as I sat pondering in mine heart I was caught away in the Spirit of the Lord . . . the Spirit said unto me: Behold, what desirest thou? And I said: I desire to behold the things which my father saw." (1 Nephi 11:1-3.) Even as an early teenager this struck me as a restatement of the desire of my heart. I wanted to have some of the religious experiences that my father had had. Since that moment I have always felt a special kinship with Nephi.

Nephi was given the vision that his father had been given. The mother of our Lord was shown to him by person, name, and mission.

Mary, like her son Jesus Christ, was prepared, chosen and foreordained before this world for the part she was destined to play in the great plan of salvation. Hers was the commission to provide a temporal body for the Lord. Hers was to cherish him in infancy and youth. Hers was to aid him in preparing for that great mission which he alone could perform. She was unquestionably one of the most noble and one of the greatest of all the offspring of the Father.

Nephi records his seeing Mary six hundred years prior to her birth on earth. "And it came to pass that I looked and beheld the great city of Jerusalem, and also other cities. And I beheld the city of Nazareth; and in the city of Nazareth I beheld a virgin, and she was exceedingly fair and white. . . . And an angel . . . said unto me: Nephi, what beholdest thou? And I said unto him: A virgin, most beautiful and fair above all other virgins." (1 Nephi 11:13-15.)

The angel then put this question to Nephi: "Knowest thou the condescension of God?" (1 Nephi 11:16.) Nephi did not know the answer, but he wanted the angel to know he knew some answers even if he did not know this precise answer. He said, "I know that he loveth his children; nevertheless, I do not know the meaning of all things." (1 Nephi 11:17.)

Nephi continues: "I beheld that she was carried away in the Spirit; and after she had been carried away in the Spirit for a space of a time the angel spake unto me, saying: Look! And I looked and beheld the virgin again, bearing a child in her arms. And the angel said unto me: Behold the Lamb of God, yea, even the Son of the Eternal Father!" (1 Nephi 11:19-21.) The scriptures tell of both the conception and the birth. It is written that Mary "conceived by the power of God."

(Mosiah 15:3.) And again, "He shall be born of Mary . . . she being a virgin, a precious and chosen vessel, who shall be overshadowed and conceive by the power of the Holy Ghost, and bring forth a son, yea, even the Son of God." (Alma 7:10.)

The angel Gabriel told Mary that her child would be "the Son of the Highest." (Luke 1:32.) Nephi's visitant explained explicitly: "Behold, the virgin whom thou seest is the mother of the Son of God, *after the manner of the flesh.*" (1 Nephi 11:18; italics added.)

It was thus that the angel answered his own question to Nephi: "Knowest thou the condescension of God?" (1 Nephi 11:16.) The condescension of God the Eternal Father is that this perfected and glorified Personage condescended to become the literal father of a son of a mortal woman.

While the Holy Ghost rested upon Mary, she gave forth one of the greatest songs of praise in the scriptures.

> And Mary said, My soul doth magnify the Lord,
> And my spirit hath rejoiced in God my Saviour.
> For he hath regarded the low estate of his handmaiden: for, behold, from henceforth all generations shall call me blessed.
> For he that is mighty hath done to me great things; and holy is his name.
> And his mercy is on them that fear him from generation to generation.
> He hath shewed strength with his arm; he hath scattered the proud in the imagination of their hearts.
> He hath put down the mighty from their seats, and exalted them of low degree.
> He hath filled the hungry with good things; and the rich he hath sent empty away.
> He hath holpen his servant Israel, in remembrance of his mercy;
> And he spake to our fathers, to Abraham, and to his seed for ever. (Luke 1:46-55.)

The most famous and far-reaching angelic visitation in recorded history serves to bring forth the superlative type of person Mary was. Let us read and ponder. "And in the sixth month the angel Gabriel was sent from God unto a city of Galilee, named Nazareth, to a virgin espoused to a man whose name was Joseph, of the house of David; and the virgin's name was Mary. And the angel came in unto her, and said, Hail, thou that art highly favoured, the Lord is with thee: blessed art thou among women." (Luke 1:26-28.)

Here we have a mighty angel appearing to a fourteen- or fifteen-year-old girl. We assume the age (inasmuch as this was the age a girl would customarily be engaged to be married in that period and culture). The angel's salutation was in Hebrew idiom, meaning, "Hello, you are the greatest and most favored girl ever born."

"And when she saw him, she was troubled at his saying, and cast in her mind what manner of salutation this should be." (Luke 1:29.) This seems to me to be the greatest understatement of the entire scriptures. I just assume she stood amazed at the circumstances.

"And the angel said unto her, Fear not, Mary: for thou hast found favour with God. And, behold, thou shalt conceive in thy womb, and bring forth a son, and shalt call his name Jesus. He shall be great, and shall be called the Son of the Highest: and the Lord God shall give unto him the throne of his father David: And he shall reign over the house of Jacob for ever; and of his kingdom there shall be no end." (Luke 1:30-33.)

Remember, this young girl is being visited by an angel, and she has never sexually known a man. A modern young lady might well try to imagine herself in such a circumstance. The message was almost incomprehensible. Mary's response was remarkably composed and simple. "Then said Mary unto the angel, How shall this be, seeing I know not a man?" (Luke 1:34.)

"And the angel answered and said unto her, The Holy Ghost shall come upon thee, and the *power of the Highest shall overshadow thee: therefore also that holy thing which shall be born of thee shall be called the Son of God*. . . . For with God nothing shall be impossible." (Luke 1:35, 37; italics added.)

Try to capture the substance and spirit of Mary's initial response. Under the trauma of these unprecedented and inexplicable circumstances and message, listen to Mary. Her perfect character is here exemplified. All of her preparations seem to unite in her response: "And Mary said, *Behold the handmaid of the Lord; be it unto me according to thy word*." (Luke 1:38; italics added.)

It seems to me that there have been three great representative and exemplary responses in holy writ. The first is found in the glimpse of the dim past before the world was. It was revealed to Moses, but made new to us through Joseph Smith. It is heard in the voice of Jesus in the councils of heaven, saying to the Father, "Here am I, send me" (Abraham 3:27), and "Father, thy will be done, and the glory be thine forever." (Moses 4:2.) His response is perfect.

Second is an account coming from the early days of this mortal world. Eve and Adam called upon God, and he gave them commandments. They were to worship him and to offer the firstlings of their flocks for an offering unto him. An angel appeared and asked: "Why dost thou offer sacrifices unto the Lord? And Adam said unto him: *I know not, save the Lord commanded me."* (Moses 5:6; italics added.) This is the perfect example for mankind — unquestioned obedience to the Lord. In this response Adam spoke as we all should speak. He was man at his best.

Finally we have Mary, the handmaid of the Almighty. Her response to the Lord's angelic messenger was the perfect model. *"Behold the handmaid of the Lord; be it unto me according to thy word."* (Luke 1:38; italics added.) Mary is woman at her best.

In the two mortal responses we have obedience with only partial understanding. This is the response of true faith.

5

Exemplary Women of the Book of Mormon

The Book of Mormon is an abridged account of God's dealings with the ancient inhabitants of the American continents from about 2250 B.C. to A.D. 421. It contains not only the Nephite records but also the Book of Ether, an abridgement of the history of the Jaredites who went to America from Asia at the time of the Tower of Babel. The original records, which were compiled and abridged to form the present book, were written on metal plates.

> These records preserved a true knowledge of God, of the mission and ministry of his Son, and of the doctrines and ordinances of salvation. Incidental to those gospel truths much information was also preserved relative to the history, and the social, . . . cultural, . . . and other conditions [of the] peoples.
>
> During the latter part of the 4th century A.D., Mormon, a prophet-general, made a compilation and abridgment of the records of [his] people. . . . [His] son Moroni added a few words of his own . . . and also abridged, in very brief form, the records of another [civilization] who had migrated to America at the time of the confusion of tongues. (Bruce R. McConkie, *Mormon Doctrine*, page 98.)

The Book of Mormon is such an abbreviated account, and so doctrinally oriented, that it does not contain much information about the lives of women. In this it is much more like the New Testament than the Old Testament. The New Testament and the Book of Mormon are the two great witnesses for Christ. Their emphasis is his witness. The personalities bearing this witness are incidental. Thus, in the New Testament account of Jesus at Jacob's well we are not told the name of the woman of Samaria. We know that she perceived that he was the promised Messiah (see John 4:25-29); "and many of the Samaritans of that city believed on him for the saying of the woman, which testified. . . ." (John 4:39.) This is a tribute to the spiritual sensitivity of the woman; but the message was her witness. So it is with the Book of Mormon. It is the message, not the personalities, that is important in this shortened account.

However, it is impossible to have even an abridged account of God's dealings with his children without talking of some women.

Sariah, Pioneer Mother of America

Sariah was the wife of Lehi and the mother of Nephi, five other sons, and several daughters. "*Sariah* is obviously Hebrew. It is a name of extreme beauty and force. Its roots are in Sara, a princess, and Jah or Iah, Jehovah, thus meaning a princess of Jehovah; a most fitting name for the mother of a multitude of nations." (George Reynolds and Janne M. Sjodahl, *Commentary on the Book of Mormon*, 6 volumes [Deseret Book Co., 1955], 1:14.)

Sariah is mentioned five times by name in the Book of Mormon account. Four of her sons — Laman, Lemuel, Sam, and Nephi — were grown to manhood before Sariah and Lehi and their family left Jerusalem, approximately 600 B.C. Two more sons — Jacob and Joseph — "were born during the little company's eight years' journey in the wilderness. When Sariah's daughters were born is very uncertain; they are not spoken of at the time [the family] left Jerusalem," and their births were not recorded in the following abbreviated account. We are told that Sariah and Lehi were well stricken in years some nine or ten years after they left Jerusalem. "It is [thus] quite possible that [Sariah's] daughters were born at Jerusalem." (George Reynolds and Janne M. Sjodahl, *Commentary on the Book of Mormon*, page 14.)

The words of Nephi typify the faith Sariah must have displayed when father Lehi was commanded to leave his wealth and means and travel in the wilderness: "I will go and do the things which the Lord hath commanded, for I know that the Lord giveth no commandments unto the children of men, save he shall prepare a way for them that they may accomplish the thing which he commandeth them." (1 Nephi 3:7.)

The lot of Sariah and her pioneer brood was not easy. Again, to apply the words of her son, "I was led by the Spirit, not knowing beforehand the things which I should do." (1 Nephi 4:6.) This type of walking by faith is difficult at best. Sariah "was exceedingly glad" when the purposes of the Lord successfully unfolded. It is true that Nephi wrote: "She also had complained against my father, telling him that he was a visionary man; saying: Behold thou hast led us forth from the land of our inheritance, and my sons are no more, and we perish in the wilderness. And after this manner of language had my mother complained against my father." (1 Nephi 5:1, 2-3.) But this was at a time of great stress and worry and loneliness in the wilderness, when she feared greatly that her four sons might have perished. When those sons returned from Jerusalem with their mission completed she was immensely strengthened in faith and bore an eloquent testimony to her husband's prophetic calling. Despite the rigors of the eight-year sojourn in the wilderness, during which time she bore at least two children, and the sorrows and stresses incident to the wickedness of her two older sons, the Book of Mormon makes no mention of her ever again questioning her husband's prophetic calling or wavering in her faith.

The Daughters of Ishmael

Ishmael was a righteous Israelite of the tribe of Ephraim. (See *Journal of Discourses*, 23:184.) In his household in Jerusalem in 600 B.C. he had five daughters and two sons. Following the promptings of the Spirit, "the sons of Lehi returned from their encampment on the borders of the Red Sea to Jerusalem and invited Ishmael and his family to join them in their journey to a promised land." (George Reynolds and Janne M. Sjodahl, *Commentary on the Book of Mormon*, 1:23.) The Lord prepared the hearts of this good family, and they accepted the invitation. (See 1 Nephi 7:3-5.)

Soon after the arrival of the family at the tents of Lehi, the eldest daughter of Ishmael was married to Zoram, a former servant of Laban and friend of Nephi who had joined in the trek, and the four other daughters of Ishmael wedded the sons of Lehi.

"And it came to pass that I, Nephi, took one of the daughters of Ishmael to wife; and also, my brethren took of the daughters of

Ishmael to wife; and also Zoram took the eldest daughter of Ishmael to wife." (1 Nephi 16:7.)

The record indicates that the sons of Ishmael never had much faith in the prophetic mission of Lehi nor in the predicted calamities to befall Jerusalem. " . . . The sons of Ishmael did begin to murmur exceedingly, because of their sufferings and afflictions in the wilderness." (1 Nephi 16:20.) The daughters who married Nephi, Sam, and Zoram apparently were receptive to the promptings of the Spirit.

Nephi records: "I, Nephi, had been blessed of the Lord exceedingly." (1 Nephi 16:8.) We are led to conclude that Nephi's wife was like Nephi, and that as a result they were compatible companions. Through them and others who followed Nephi's leadership a righteous nation was reared to the Lord.

Thus the record shows the family of a righteous, God-fearing man being approached by the sons of Lehi. For all we know, the young men may even have been strangers to Ishmael's family, but they were on the Lord's errand. The parents' and daughters' hearts were softened toward the young men, and although we have no record of their courtship, the family joined Lehi and his family in its great pilgrimage to the Americas.

In all of this, three of the daughters of Ishmael seemed to sense the truth that they could find fulfillment in marriage to righteous men who were engaged in God's purposes. Apparently they knew that they could attain contentment and meaning in their lives by being wives and mothers. In this they are proper models. These faithful daughters must have known that they were — to use a Book of Mormon phrase — to "raise up seed unto [God]." (Jacob 2:30.)

Lehi and Ishmael were cut from the same cloth. The Lord could safely raise up a righteous generation through some of Ishmael's daughters and Lehi's sons. One of the pleasures of pondering the Book of Mormon is to relive the joy of the parents as Father Lehi called his grandchildren around him: " . . . Behold, my sons, and my daughters, who are the sons and daughters of my first-born. . . . I cannot go down to my grave save I should leave a blessing upon you; for behold, I know that if ye are brought up in the way ye should go ye will not depart from it. . . . I leave my blessing upon you. . . . he spake unto Sam, saying: Blessed art thou, and thy seed; for thou shalt inherit the land like unto thy brother Nephi. . . . And thou shalt be blessed in all thy days." (2 Nephi 4:3, 5-6, 11.) The blessings of heaven attend those who live the commandments. And those blessings are naturally attracted to families wherein the wives and mothers are women of faith such as we assume the girls were who married Zoram, Nephi, and Sam.

Abish the Convert and the Queen

Two women were instrumental in commencing the work of conversion among the Lamanites which eventually brought many thousands of persons into the Church.

With other Nephite missionaries, Ammon entered Lamanite territory intent on such conversions. In the land of Ishmael, Lamoni was the king. Captured and taken before Lamoni, Ammon found favor with the king and was assigned with a group of Lamanites to take care of the king's flock. This he did with such marvelous strength and power in preventing a robber band from scattering and stealing the flocks that the king, on hearing the report of this action, was overawed and reduced to silence. Surely, he thought, Ammon must be the Great Spirit.

"And it came to pass that Ammon, being filled with the Spirit of God, therefore he perceived the thoughts of the king. . . . I say unto you, what is it, that thy marvelings are so great? Behold, I am a man, and am thy servant. . . . Now when the king had heard these words, he marveled again, for he beheld that Ammon could discern his thoughts." (Alma 18:16-18.)

From this position of strength Ammon taught King Lamoni about God and man: " . . . Man in the beginning was created after the image of God." (Alma 18:34.) He now unfolded the plan of salvation to Lamoni whose rapture at having this precious knowledge revealed to him all at once was more than he could contain, and "he fell unto the earth, as if he were dead." (Alma 18:42.)

His servants took him to his wife, and she had him laid upon a bed. He remained in this condition for two days and two nights. His wife and sons and daughters mourned over him as though he were dead. After this time they were about to take him to the sepulchre for burial.

The queen summoned Ammon. Was the king dead? she asked. "He is not dead," said Ammon, "but he sleepeth in God, and on the morrow he shall rise again." She intuitively accepted Ammon as a prophet: "I have had no witness save thy word, and the word of our servants; nevertheless I believe that it shall be according as thou hast said." (Alma 19:8-9.)

Ammon blessed this good woman because of her faith: "Woman, there has not been such great faith among all the people of the Nephites." (Alma 19:10.) According to Ammon's promise, the next day Lamoni arose and "stretched forth his hand unto the woman, and he said: Blessed be the name of God, and blessed art thou." (Alma 19:12.)

Lamoni followed a pattern of those who accept the gospel truths: he praised God and blessed his faithful wife. Wives are beneficiaries when their husbands are magnified.

King Lamoni then taught his wife until they were both "over-powered by the Spirit." (Alma 19:13.) It was a time of exquisite emotion and they sunk down with joy. Finally, husband, wife, and Ammon — the messenger from God — "all three... sunk to the earth." (Alma 19:14.)

The servants, seeing what had happened, also began to call on God. They accepted the witness of the Spirit and were overcome also.

Only one servant was not overcome, a woman named Abish whose father had been given a remarkable vision some time before. Abish had "been converted unto the Lord for many years" but had not made her conversion known to her peers. She understood the work-ings of the Spirit and "knew that it was the power of God" that had caused Lamoni and the others to fall to the earth. (See Alma 19:16-17.) Abish seized upon this as the teaching moment to bring others into the Church. She ran from house to house, telling the people what had happened.

When the aroused people assembled, a contention arose. When some saw the prostrate form of Ammon, the Nephite, with those of their king and queen, they assumed an evil had come upon the king and his house. Others disagreed. Some "said that Ammon was the Great Spirit [or]... was sent by the Great Spirit;... And thus the contention began to be exceeding sharp among them." (Alma 19:25, 28.)

Abish was sorrowful because of the comments. "She went and took the queen by the hand, that perhaps she might raise her from the ground; and as soon as she touched her hand [the queen] arose and stood upon her feet, and cried with a loud voice, saying:... O blessed God, have mercy on this people!" (Alma 19:29.) The queen took her husband by the hand, and he arose and stood on his feet.

We thus see the important roles a sensitive, faithful wife and a courageous, converted servant woman played in accomplishing God's purposes. It is written: "... And as many as did believe were baptized; and they became a righteous people, and they did establish a church among them. And thus the work of the Lord did commence among the Lamanites." (Alma 19:35-36.)

The Mothers of the Stripling Ammonites

The Lamanities who were converted to Christianity through the instrumentality of Ammon were called Ammonites by the Nephites. These converts were indeed born again. " . . . They took their swords, and all the weapons which were used for the shedding of man's blood, and they did bury them deep in the earth . . . . covenanting with God, that rather than shed the blood of their brethren they would give up their own lives." (Alma 24:17-18.) They were true to this covenant, and many of them gave up their lives because of it.

Eventually wisdom dictated that they migrate to the lands of the Nephites. The Nephites greeted them warmly, and they lived among them in peace and brotherhood. When the Lamanite armies marched against them, the Nephites protected them.

Over a period of time these converts considered breaking their covenant because of the loss of life suffered by their Nephite brethren in their protection. But their prophet, Helaman, "feared lest by so doing they should lose their souls." (Alma 53:15.)

Because the young sons of these good people had not entered into the covenant not to fight, they joined the army and served together as a unit. It appears that these boys were nearly all teenagers. "Helaman did march at the head of his two thousand stripling soldiers." (Alma 53:22.) In reporting to his commanding officer, Helaman referred to his troops as "my two thousand sons, (for they are worthy to be called sons)." (Alma 56:10.)

During a forced march by both Lamanite and Nephite armies, Helaman called a hasty council of war. He explained to his "sons" that if the enemy was to be trapped, his unit would be under the necessity of joining the battle against the Lamanite troops. The untested youngsters would meet seasoned warriors in battle. He put it to them: "Therefore what say ye, my sons, will ye go against them to battle? (Alma 56:44.) The answer of these "very young" soldiers was such that Helaman said afterwards that he had never seen such courage. They said to him: " . . . Father, behold our God is with us, and he will not suffer that we should fall; then let us go forth; we would not slay our brethren if they would let us alone; therefore, let us go, lest they should overpower the [Nephite] army." (Alma 56:46.)

As history records, they did go forth, and they carried the battle. Their people were saved from extinction, and God was with them in a most miraculous way: " . . . Not one soul of them [fell] to the earth; yea, and they had fought as if with the strength of God; yea, never were men known to have fought with such miraculous strength." (Alma 56:56.)

Even their prophet-leader could hardly understand the source of their courage. It is in his written report to the commanding general, Moroni, that we find one of the greatest tributes ever recorded to women. "Now they never had fought, yet they did not fear death; and they did think more upon the liberty of their fathers than they did upon their lives; yea, *they had been taught by their mothers, that if they did not doubt, God would deliver them.* (Alma 56:47; italics added.)

In examining the source of the strength and courage of these young men the prophet found it to be in their mothers. This is an eternal truth. Here it is dramatically emphasized. Listen to the children's praise rise to the heavens themselves! *"And they rehearsed unto me the words of their mothers, saying; We do not doubt our mothers knew it."* (Alma 56:48; italics added.)

None of these young men wanted to fight and kill, and their mothers certainly did not desire it. But they knew the Lord's instructions to the Nephites, that one of the causes that may justify bloodshed is self-defense. As stated in the Book of Mormon, "the Lord has said that: Ye shall defend your families even unto bloodshed." (Alma 43:47.)

When the resurrected Jesus appeared to the Nephite people, he instructed them: "Pray in your families unto the Father, always in my name, that your wives and your children may be blessed." (3 Nephi 18:21.) Families and child rearing are of inestimable worth. In large measure, as with the exemplary women from the Book of Mormon, mothers fashion the children. To this end fathers are under divine direction to bless their wives and children.

One of the best illustrations of what a proper model may accomplish is the case of the mothers of the stripling soldiers. It is a classic example of a mother sharing the gospel with her family.

6

Assault on the Family

Among the Saints the family is the basic unit. It is the fundamental part of the Church. Its needs and preservation should take precedence over all other activities and things. "An ultimate goal of quorum presidencies and their representatives (priesthood home teachers) is to inspire... the family to conform to all Church standards, including honesty, morality.... The family is the basic unit of the Church and of society." (*Melchizedek Priesthood Handbook* [Salt Lake City: The Church of Jesus Christ of Latter-day Saints, 1975], pages 11, 17.)

" 'There must be a union of those who cannot exist without each other,' Aristotle writes, 'namely, of male and female, that the race may continue.... Mankind have a natural desire to leave behind them an image of themselves.' " (Mortimer J. Adler, ed., *The Great Ideas, A Syntopticon of Great Books of the Western World*, 2 volumes [Chicago: Encyclopaedia Britannica, Inc., 1952], 1:487.)

The United States Supreme Court has held in a series of cases that marriage and the rearing of a family are fundamental civil rights of man. This highest of civil tribunals concludes: "The parents' claim to authority in their own household to direct the rearing of their children is basic in the structure of our society." (*Ginsberg* v. *New York*, 390 U.S. 629 1968.)

The human infant requires years of care in order to survive. If the family (normally, a wife, husband, and their children) did not exist as a relatively stable organization to serve the purpose, some other social agency would have to provide sustained care for children. Wherever civilization has been found, some form of family has existed. The procreation and rearing of offspring is the function which the family naturally exists to perform.

Children are the bond of the marriage union which makes the family a community. Hegel writes:

> The relation of love between husband and wife is in itself not objective, because even if their feeling is their substantial unity, still this unity has no objectivity. Such an objectivity parents first acquire in their children, in whom they can see objectified the entirety of their union. In the child, a mother loves its father and he its mother. Both have their love objectified for them in the child. While in their goods their unity is embodied only in an external thing, in their children it is embodied in a spiritual one in which the parents are loved and which they love. (Mortimer J. Adler, *The Great Ideas*, 1:487.)

As we have previously discussed, the Saints consider marriage to be not only natural and a fundamental right but also a divine institution; it was ordained by God himself in the paradise of the Garden of Eden and confirmed by Jesus Christ. So also is the fruit of marriage — the family. The family here should be patterned after "the family in heaven." (Ephesians 3:15.) Earthly families are to follow heavenly concepts: "that which is temporal in the likeness of that which is spiritual." (D&C 77:2.)

The Church itself is a service unit for the family. "The Church helps us to create and perfect eternal family units; it serves the family and the individual." (*General Handbook of Instructions*, number 21 [The Church of Jesus Christ of Latter-day Saints], page 96.) The Church protects and serves not only individuals but the family. Many Church programs are scheduled for the benefit of the family, and the Church serves as a resource for parents. For instance,

> To aid parents in holding weekly family home evening with their children, Monday evening has been designated in the Church to be kept free of ward or stake activities. The family home evening manual is written as an aid to meet the needs of every Latter-day Saint. Members should be counseled to retain their manuals from year to year. Some of the contents may be more useful at one time than another. (*General Handbook*, page 96.)

Ideally, there should be no conflict between Church programs and the family. By scriptural definition the Church is its membership. "Behold, this is my doctrine — whosoever repenteth and cometh unto me, the same is my church." (D&C 10:67.) The family is a Church unit. "As a Church unit, a family has a presiding officer. . . . Therefore, when properly functioning in the home with the priesthood, the father is the basic priesthood officer in the Church." (*Melchizedek Priesthood Handbook,* page 17.) The Lord has declared his purpose: "For behold, this is my work and my glory — to bring to pass the immortality and eternal life of man." (Moses 1:39.) The families and the larger Church are to make God's work their own. There is, thus, unity of purpose.

Every day the application of these noble principles brings seeming conflicts of interest. What is the correct balance between a wife's desire to perform Church service and her desire to her husband and family? When does a father and husband put children and wife before his response to Church callings? These are constant problems in the real world. They can only be answered by prayerful attention to each problem as it arises. Understanding gospel principles and following the advice of the Brethren can provide some guidelines.

First: Salvation is a family affair. Those who participate in the fulness of salvation do so in family units. (See 1 Corinthians 11:11; D&C 132:15-17.) Positions held and even meritorious services rendered will not compensate in the eternal scheme of things for lack of full effort to save the immediate family.

Many busy husbands have on occasion come home from a taxing day's work and been tempted to say, when they've seen the physical and emotional effort necessary to care for tired children, "I've got a Church meeting to go to." Many have succumbed to the temptation to escape, using the rationalization that they were doing a virtuous service.

If there comes a bona fide choice between family and any other activity, the family should take precedence.

Second: "And see that all these things are done in wisdom and order; for it is not requisite that a man should run faster than he has strength." (Mosiah 4:27.) Don't let the things that matter most be at the mercy of things that matter less. We often have to make choices from among things that are each "good."

Third: The Saints view celestial marriage here in mortality as beginning an eternal family. It is through celestial marriage that the faithful continue in family units in eternity. (See D&C 131:1-4; 132:16-32.) Perfect peace and a full endowment of all good graces attend such eternal families. All decisions affecting the family should be made with this in mind.

Lucifer, or to use his Hebrew name, Satan, "became a devil, having sought that which was evil before God." (2 Nephi 2:17.) It is written of him that he was a liar from the beginning. He has placed himself in eternal opposition to the divine will. "Wherefore, because that Satan rebelled against me, ... I caused that he should be cast down; and he became Satan, yea, even the devil, the father of all lies, to deceive and to blind men, and to lead them captive at his will, even as many as would not hearken unto my voice." (Moses 4:3-4.)

The devil desires to tempt and entice men and women to leave the path of truth and walk in darkness. He is the enemy of God and the divine order. Jesus said of him, "The enemy . . . is the devil." (Matthew 13:39.) It is to be expected that he would unloose an assault upon the divine order of the family. Indeed, in the philosophy of opposites he advocates every principle that is in opposition to the order of a heavenly family.

The devil uses many tools in his efforts to corrupt a marriage. Some of these are divorce, birth control, abortion, fornication, adultery, masturbation, and homosexuality. All of these are assaults upon the family.

Corruption of Marriage

The falling away from marriage as defined by God may be explained in four phases: apostasy brought the loss of authority to act for and in behalf of God; the correct form or concept of marriage was lost; the meaning and responsibilities, the substance was lost; the relationships between the husband and wife and between them and God were changed.

God himself performed the first marriage before death entered into the world. It was an eternal marriage. This type of union has been the Lord's order in all ages when his authorized agents have been upon the earth. Whenever there has been the fulness of the gospel, there has been God's type and quality of marriage — celestial marriage. Celestial marriages are performed pursuant to the sealing powers of God.

> The participating parties become husband and wife in this mortal life, and if after their marriage they keep all the terms and conditions of this order of the priesthood, they continue on as husband and wife in the celestial kingdom of God. If the family unit continues, then by virtue of that fact the members of the family have gained eternal life (exaltation), the greatest of all the gifts of God,

for by definition, exaltation consists in the continuation of the family unit in eternity. (Bruce R. McConkie, *Mormon Doctrine*, page 117; see also Joseph Fielding Smith, *Doctrines of Salvation*, 2:58-99.)

"[Since Adam and Eve, and their prototype of marriage], to the present, the whole history of the world has been one recurring instance of personal and group *apostasy* after another." God married Adam and Eve and gave to them the fulness of the gospel "so that all matters pertaining to this mortal sphere could be governed and arranged in harmony with the order of heaven. Apostasy consists in the abandonment and forsaking of these true principles. . . .

"The Lord's handdealings with men [and women] have always been designed to keep the faithful from the treason of apostasy and to encourage those who do not have the fulness of truth to come to the light" (Bruce R. McConkie, *Mormon Doctrine*, page 43) and to the ordinances of salvation, including marriage. It is thus that Isaiah quotes the Lord as saying:

Forasmuch as this people draw near me with their mouth, and with their lips do honour me, but have removed their heart far from me, and their fear toward me is taught by the precept of men: . . . (Isaiah 29:13.)

Paul foretold of "perilous times" that would come "in the last days"; times when men would have "a form of godliness," but they would deny "the power thereof." (See 2 Timothy 3:1, 5.)

It is the belief of Latter-day Saints that the prophesied falling away from the truth has occurred. Through apostasy men lost the power and authority to act in God's name.

As persons lost the power of God, they changed the form of the marriage he had instituted. Thus the marriage ordinance has been corrupted into a temporal contract only. It is now virtually universal practice to say in the performance of a marriage ceremony "till death do you part." The apostate notion of temporary marriage unions changes the whole concept of marriage. It is a part of the devil's attack on God's order of things.

With this change in form come fundamental changes in attitudes about the nature of the marriage union and substantive changes in the marriage itself. If marriage is to be viewed as a contract lasting only a few years, how few? The seeds of divorce tend to be sown in the marriage ceremony itself.

If a husband and wife view their marriage as an eternal covenant, there is a natural built-in emphasis on problem-solving and building the marriage. The breaking up of the union is less likely to be seen as a viable alternative. Fulfillment, not breach, is the order. If marriage is viewed as a temporary arrangement, however, changing partners may seem easier and more desirable than personality and character adjustment of the two parties.

When the contracting parties are accountable to God for the proper fulfillment of the covenants, responsibilities are deeper than when the contracting parties are only accountable to themselves and to each other. If the family unit is to be projected into the eternities, parents' responsibilities to children are much more comprehensive than if their responsibilities are limited to nurturing and caring for children until they reach maturity.

When the purpose of a marriage and family is limited, resilience and permanency in that marriage and family are diminished.

Apostasy has also brought a changing of the relations among the contracting parties. I say *among* instead of *between* because in God's order of marriage there are three persons involved in the marriage covenant: God, the woman, and the man. When God makes a covenant, it is forever. When he is taken out of it, the sacred covenant becomes a mortal contract. (See D&C 132:7.) When the marriage contract is reduced to a two-party agreement, it carries with it the infirmities of all two-party instruments: the tendency toward misinterpretation and breach.

With the nuptial contract made a two-party instead of a three-party instrument, the relationship of the wife and husband changes. Historically, it can be demonstrated that both parties have suffered because of this change from the true order, women suffering more grievously because of the husband's frequently unrighteous dominion. Roles have been improperly and narrowly construed and the purpose and quality of celestial marriage has suffered because of the evils of apostasy.

As her stake president I had a young wife complain to me about her husband. She had so many uncomplimentary things to say about him that I tried to get some positive response as a beginning point for some reconstruction. "Is there anything of worth that your husband does?" I inquired. Then this response came with a touch of bitterness: "Oh, yes, he stands around and holds his priesthood!" That husband, notwithstanding the potential power within him, had become immersed in apostate traditions. Indeed, false concepts had been reinforced because of his lack of understanding about the role of a priesthood bearer.

In a celestial marriage the contracting woman and man are

partners. They owe one another the same obligations of love, respect, and fidelity. They share responsibilities to their children. Each assumes the obligation and accountability for fulfilling and enlarging both self and spouse. No contract is self-executing. People are obliged to perform, to function, to work to make the relationship operate to the benefit of the concerned parties. The contract of marriage is meant to establish a unity between the wife and the husband.

Partners in an enterprise do not necessarily have identical responsibilities. There may be a division of labor. One partner may best make one contribution and the other partner another. In a business organization one partner may contribute money and funds to the partnership while another may contribute talent or labor, yet both might share equally in the benefits. One may manage and one perform otherwise. Still, it is a valid partnership.

As marriage is a religious ordinance as well as a contract, scriptures help us understand the relationship of the interested parties. "Husbands, love your wives, even as Christ also loved the church, and gave himself for it. . . . So ought men to love their wives as their own bodies." (Ephesians 5:25, 28.) This is the first law in God's order of marriage. The apostle Paul, in teaching celestial marriage, reiterates what God related in the Garden of Eden: "For this cause shall a man leave his father and mother, and shall be joined unto his wife, and they two shall be one flesh." He continues with the first principle of marriage: "Nevertheless let every one of you in particular so love his wife even as himself." (Ephesians 5:31, 33.)

This inspired apostle of God understood that proper love of wife helps to magnify a husband. "He that loveth his wife loveth himself," he said. (Ephesians 5:28.) As the marriage union is enhanced, so the participants are enlarged and fulfilled. It is a deterioration from the standard for one party to suppose that she or he has a primary duty to herself or himself. The gospel of marriage anticipates that the husband and wife give themselves to one another. Each finds unity and new life by living outside himself. Individual fulfillment is found in building the marriage and the family. Using Christ's teachings as an example, we recall that he said, "He that findeth his life shall lose it." (Matthew 10:39.) Selfishness has no place in celestial marriage. Spouses who love each other best, love themselves. They have a self-respect which enables them to respect one another.

The scriptural role of the wife is given in terms with a shade different meaning: ". . . and the wife see that she reverence her husband." (Ephesians 5:33.)

When there is an absence of "love" and "reverence" between a husband and wife, the marriage is "corrupted" to the extent of that absence.

The Christian husband is under scriptural obligation to support his wife and children under normal circumstances. "But if any provide not for his own, and specially for those of his own house, he hath denied the faith, and is worse than an infidel." (1 Timothy 5:8.)

Peter, the chief of the Lord's apostles, gave insight into the proper relationship in the marriage covenant. To be understood, his words should be read in the light of the division of labor and responsibility in the marriage partnership agreement. Peter recorded:

> Likewise, ye wives, be in subjection to your own husbands; . . . while they behold your chaste conversation coupled with fear. Whose adorning let it not be that outward adorning. . . . But let it be the hidden man of the heart, in that which is not corruptible, even the ornament of a meek and quiet spirit, which is in the sight of God of great price. For after this manner in the old time the holy women also, who trusted in God, adorned themselves, being in subjection unto their own husbands: Even as Sara obeyed Abraham, calling him lord: whose daughters ye are, as long as ye do well, and are not afraid with any amazement."(1 Peter 3:1-6.)

Sara was never called upon to respond to an unrighteous Abraham. It is presupposed that a wife is to be subject to her husband only in righteousness.

It is in this sense that Paul says: "Wives, submit yourselves unto your own husbands, as unto the Lord. For the husband is the head of the wife, even as Christ is the head of the church. . . . Therefore as the church is subject unto Christ, so let the wives be to their own husbands in every thing." (Ephesians 5:22-24.)

Christ is the sole perfect exemplar. He never exercised unrighteous dominion. He taught and lived the rule of love. (See John 14:15, 23-24.) In a celestial marriage relationship husbands and wives should be in perfect harmony, as Christ is to his church. There is to be no usurpation. It was Christ who said: "But he that is greatest among you shall be your servant. And whosoever shall exalt himself shall be abased; and he that shall humble himself shall be exalted." (Matthew 23:11-12.)

This is not just the Christian way; it is *the* way.

The marriage and the home should be an institution of law and order. There is no order without law. Any wife who fails to accord a righteous husband deference for his position as head of the household, and who disparages him in the eyes of her children, will live to regret her actions. Also, any man who heads a household who does not make himself worthy of the respect of his wife and children will be sorry. Mutual relationship can and should be maintained without the least impairment of the concept of partnership in marriage.

And what is the wife's portion in all this? Peter continues, "Likewise, ye husbands, dwell with them according to knowledge, giving honour unto the wife . . . and as being heirs together of the grace of life." (1 Peter 3:7.) The husband honors the wife. He takes her counsel. He respects and heeds her advice. He recognizes her as truly a partner. The wife is a joint heir with her husband. That is, they are as one here and hereafter. They lead the children in a joint venture. Neither the wife nor the husband can have ultimate fulfillment separately. "Neither is the man without the woman, neither the woman without the man, in the Lord." (1 Corinthians 11:11.)

Any action, great or small, that detracts from this ultimate unity with the Lord, tends to corrupt the marriage.

Divorce

The gospel has made great contributions to the solidarity and well-being of the home. It furnishes the basic concepts upon which this sacred institution is built. Through gospel instruction we learn that marriage is ordained by the Lord; that marriages should be eternal in duration; that marriages are charged with a primary responsibility for receiving in tabernacles of flesh the spirit children of the Father; that these spirits are to be nurtured and trained in mortality; and, finally, that the wife, husband, and children have the opportunity to return to the presence of God whence they came.

In God's system of things there should be no divorce. Since it brings the dissolution of a marriage it may be viewed as the ultimate corruption of marriage. However, "since all men — as a result of apostasy and iniquity — are not living . . . the full and perfect gospel law, the Lord permits divorce and allows the dissolution of the marriage union." (Bruce R. McConkie, *Mormon Doctrine*, page 203.)

In various dispensations the Lord allowed divorce in circumstances varying according to the light and knowledge given to the people.

Under the law of Moses, divorce was permitted because the people were not able to live the high gospel standard which would abolish it. (Leviticus 21:7, 12; Deuteronomy 24:1-4.) As revealed to the Jews and the Nephites, the terms of the perfect marriage system include this teaching: "It hath been written, that

whosoever shall put away his wife, let him give her a writing of
divorcement. Verily, Verily, I say unto you, that whosoever shall
put away his wife, saving for the cause of fornication, causeth her
to commit adultery; and whoso shall marry her who is divorced
committeth adultery." (3 Nephi 12:31-32; Matthew 5:31-32.)

When the Pharisees raised the divorce issue to tempt him,
our Lord taught them the eternity of the marriage covenant
("What therefore God hath joined together, let not man put asunder"), told them that Moses permitted divorce because of the
hardness of their hearts, but explained that from the beginning it
had not been so ordained. Then it appears he went into the house
and gave special and added instructions to "his disciples." For
them the law was: "Whosoever shall put away his wife, and marry
another, committeth adultery against her. And if a woman shall
put away her husband, and be married to another, she committeth
adultery." (Mark 10:2-12.) Also, to his disciples he said: "All men
cannot receive this saying, save they to whom it is given. . . . He
that is able to receive it, let him receive it." (Matthew 19:3-12;
Doctrines of Salvation, vol. 2, pp. 80-85.) [Bruce R. McConkie,
Mormon Doctrine, page 203.]

That is, Jesus taught that where people were able to live the higher,
celestial law there would be no divorce.

In this matter, then, some Church members fall short of living
the full and perfect law. The Church in effect acknowledges this to be
so. As in other matters of lifestyle, we are living a lesser law to
prepare us for the higher law. For instance, we are living the law of
tithing to prepare us for the law of consecration.

It is somewhat as it was in the days of Moses; divorce is permitted because of the hardness of the hearts of the people, and the
Lord permits his agents to exercise the power to loose as well as
the power to bind. (Bruce R. McConkie, *Mormon Doctrine,* page
204.)

The Lord's agents apparently have determined that in our present
condition there are some circumstances wherein it would be a greater
disruption in the salvation of individuals for them to live together
than for them to divorce. Thus the Church allows divorce for grounds
other than adultery, and under present Church law one who marries
a divorced person does not by that circumstance either commit adultery or cause the spouse to.

It should be noted that it is Church policy that if a marriage is
dissolved because of an illict relationship between one of the partners

and a third party, those two persons may not be sealed in celestial marriage without the special approval of the First Presidency.

As a practicing attorney I have investigated domestic problems by the score and have participated in divorce suits. Having heard the evidence of the parties concerned, as I look back over my experiences and observations I can recall few instances in which repentance from bad conduct on the part of the man or the woman or both would not have been the answer. Unfortunately, however, divorce seems to be accepted with increasing tolerance today.

As a young bishop — a common judge in Israel — I faced the domestic relations counseling that is entailed in that assignment. In that task I was given much help by the comments of a member of the First Presidency of that day, President Stephen L Richards. In a general priesthood conference he emphasized the seriousness of divorce and commented, "The remedy for domestic problems and irritations is not divorce, but repentance." (*General Conference Report,* October 1954, page 80.) Nevertheless I learned as a young bishop that it is one thing to be skillful in composing difficulties, to counsel and advise, but it is quite another thing to call to repentance.

The need for repentance, however, is universal, and is by no means confined to divorced persons. But within a marriage that need frequently is not as obvious as repentance for such things as stealing, for instance. The elements of repentance in marriage are the same as in any other circumstances. The scriptures outline them: godly sorrow (2 Corinthians 7:10); forsaking of sin (D&C 58:43; Isaiah 1:16); confession (D&C 64:7); where possible, righting the wrong by restitution (Numbers 5:7-8); living the law. "He that repents and does the commandments of the Lord shall be forgiven." (D&C 1:32; see also Oscar W. McConkie, *Aaronic Priesthood* [Deseret Book Co., 1977], pages 65-69.) It is in the final element, living the celestial law, that all of us hope to find remission of sins and become true Saints.

Birth Control

Divorce is the extreme of corruption of a marriage, but less radical developments can diminish total unity and threaten the purpose of marriage. One such is birth control.

In the public mind, *birth control* as a term has rather precise meanings: population control, the deliberate curtailing of human births, the control of the number of children and the timing of their births. It means to control conception, to limit, space, or exclude the birth of children. It is the limiting of the number of children to an unnaturally small number.

In 1831 God gave the Prophet Joseph Smith a revelation on social relationships and his purposes in the earth. It sets the tone for true and full Christian living: "But it is not given that one man should possess that which is above another, wherefore the world lieth in sin." (D&C 49:20.) In this revelation the Lord says, "Marriage is ordained of God ... that earth might answer the end of its creation; and that it might be filled with the measure of man, according to his creation before the world was made." (D&C 49:15-17.)

God thus reiterated in this last dispensation what he stated in the first and second dispensations: "Be fruitful, and multiply, and replenish the earth." (Genesis 1:28; see also Genesis 9:6-9.) In this dispensation he gives the added information that having posterity has to do with "creation before the world was." (D&C 49:17.) That is, it has to do with providing bodies for the hosts of spirits waiting to come to this earth in physical bodies.

In the old Bowery, a pioneer structure made of boughs and a thatched roof, Brigham Young made plain the meaning of the revelation just quoted. He said:

> There are multitudes of pure and holy spirits waiting to take tabernacles, now what is our duty? — to prepare tabernacles for them; to take a course that will not tend to drive those spirits into the families of the wicked, where they will be trained in wickedness, debauchery, and every species of crime. *It is the duty of every righteous man and woman to prepare tabernacles for all the spirits they can* ... that the noble spirits which are waiting for tabernacles might be brought forth. (*Journal of Discourses,* 4:56; italics added.)

Given this light and knowledge of the purpose of this earth life, the leaders of the Church have uniformly counseled against selfishly curtailing births to one or two per family. President Joseph F. Smith instructed the mothers of the Church in 1917, and, in turn, was quoted by his son who succeeded him to the presidency in 1972:

> I regret, I think it is a crying evil, that there should exist a sentiment or a feeling among any members of the Church to curtail the birth of their children ... where husband and wife are in possession of health and vigor and are free from impurities that would be entailed upon their posterity. I believe that *where people undertake to curtail or prevent the birth of their children that they are going to reap disappointment by and by.... I believe that is one of the greatest crimes of the world today, this evil practice.* (Joseph Fielding Smith, *Doctrines of Salvation,* 2:88-89.)

In February of 1971 the Church reaffirmed the applicability of this counsel. "The Church takes the view that any tampering with the fountains of life is serious, both morally and physiologically. The Lord's command imposed upon Latter-day Saints is to 'multiply and replenish the earth.' " (*Priesthood Bulletin,* February 1971 [volume 7, number 1], item 6.)

In April of 1969 the First Presidency wrote the following letter to the officers of the Church presiding over stakes, wards, and missions:

Dear Brethren:

The First Presidency is being asked from time to time as to what the attitude of the Church is regarding birth control. In order that you may be informed on this subject and that you may be prepared to convey the proper information to the members of the Church under your jurisdiction, we have decided to give you the following statement:

We seriously regret that there should exist a sentiment or feeling among any members of the Church to curtail the birth of their children. We have been commanded to multiply and re-plenish the earth that we may have joy and rejoicing in our posterity.

Where husband and wife enjoy health and vigor and are free from impurities that would be entailed upon their posterity, it is contrary to the teachings of the Church artificially to curtail or prevent the birth of children. We believe that those who practice birth control will reap disappointment by and by.

However, we feel that men must be considerate of their wives who bear the greater responsibility not only of bearing children, but of caring for them through childhood. To this end the mother's health and strength should be conserved and the husband's consideration for his wife is his first duty, and self-control a dominant factor in all their relationships.

It is our further feeling that married couples should seek inspiration and wisdom from the Lord that they may exercise discretion in solving their marital problems, and that they may be permitted to rear their children in accordance with the teachings of the gospel. (Letter of the First Presidency, April 14, 1969.)

This Church policy is based on doctrinal concepts; however, Church counsel has avoided rigidity: "The mother's health and strength should be conserved," the bodies of the children should not be "entailed" with physical impurities of the parents, the "husband's consideration for his wife is his first duty." Finally, the couple is to "seek inspiration and wisdom from the Lord" and is allowed "discretion in solving their marital problems."

All of this means to me that faithful Latter-day Saints should feel free to work out the best way to accomplish God's purposes in their particular circumstances. This does not necessarily mean that the couple should have a child every year. It just may be that in view of the health and strength of the wife, healthier children would result if the births were further apart. Each couple should feel their obligation to procreate, and the best pattern in which they should have progeny must be left to their own prayerful consideration combined with the Lord's will.

When someone asks me if the Church counsels against birth control, my response is yes. However, if someone asks me how a couple can best fulfill its obligation to have children, I will reply that there are various ways that may properly be considered. In any event, I do not think that abstinence from sexual relations within marriage is a workable alternative. That expression of love is a vital part of a fulfilling and happy marriage relationship.

The Church counsels against the voluntary limiting of children to one or two per family in normal circumstances. It affirmatively enjoins couples to have as many children as unselfish reason and circumstances permit. It warns of disappointment in the future for those who do not follow that counsel. The Church does not get involved in the means that a faithful couple may determine to preserve the health and strength of the mother in fulfilling the responsibility to have children. All sorts of planning and controls may properly be considered. Such intimate matters are wisely left to the couple's "discretion in solving marital problems," and the couple is left latitude to "rear . . . children in accordance with the teachings of the gospel."

There is a great hue and cry in this day about overpopulation. Prophets of gloom and doom are predicting that there will be too many mouths for the earth's capacity to feed. All sorts of rationalizations are given to justify worldly desire for things and possessions rather than seeking eternal fulfillment in children and children's children.

I suppose that if the earth's grain crop were used for bread rather than for beer and alcoholic beverages, if the wealth of nations were turned to peace rather than war, if grain were planted in place of tobacco or harmful drugs, and if governments and peoples turned their attention to solving the distribution problems associated with surplus and poverty, the arguments of the population explosionists would be put to rest. If we would live by God's concepts, there would be enough for all.

In our day the Lord has said:

I, the Lord, stretched out the heavens, and built the earth, my very handiwork; and all things therein are mine.

And it is my purpose to provide for my saints, for all things are mine.

But it must needs be done in mine own way. . . .

For the earth is full, and there is enough and to spare. (D&C 104:14-17.)

To the believer the word of the Lord is sufficient. The believer does not walk in fear. He delights in both the commands and the promises of the Lord.

Abortion

If birth control can be a threat to the family, what shall we say of deliberately induced abortion?

An abortion is the expulsion of a fetus from the womb before it is sufficiently developed to survive. It can occur naturally, as in the case of a miscarriage. When unlawfully induced, it is called criminal abortion.

In the early stages of pregnancy, abortions may be brought about by relatively simple surgical procedures. As a consequence, abortion is discussed among worldly people as though it were a matter of legitimate population control. But the issue of abortion is much too broad to be considered a medical matter only. In it are legal, ethical, moral, theological, and emotional overtones. Likewise it is much more than a sectarian issue, a concern that pertains to one faith alone. The basic issue of legalized abortions relates to human life, to the obligations which a responsible moral society has to human life, and to the moral agency of the interested parties.

One hears frivolous talk about the fetus in the womb being no more than a piece of tissue whose removal is as easy as, and the equivalent to, the removal of tonsils. Let us compare a tonsillectomy and an abortion through what we are told by medical persons. Both tissues are alive; both are composed of material substances, chemical compounds, and special molecules. However, there are at least three ways in which fetal tissue and tonsillectomy tissue are different.

First, fetal tissue is unique. There never was and never will be another piece of tissue identical to it. The tonsil tissue is closely related to all other tissue in the patient's body.

Second, fetal tissue is different from the parent organism. I think every biologist would say there is this difference. Your tonsils are yours and yours alone; but a mother's fetal tissue is not hers.

Third, fetal tissue has human potential. This is the primary difference. Unless molested, unless life support is interfered with or
withdrawn, human fetal tissue has the potential, the capability, and
the likelihood of developing into a human being. It is the human
potential of the fetal tissue that has moved society to set abortion
apart from other surgical procedures.

Governments have traditionally had a substantial and compelling interest in abortion statutes. As previously mentioned, the
United States Supreme Court considers such matters to be basic civil
rights of man. Both legislative bodies and courts have acknowledged
that marriage and procreation are fundamental to the very existence
and survival of the race. Population is a necessary prerequisite and an
essential characteristic of a state. This is one of a state's interests.
Governments have a legitimate interest in the health of persons within
their jurisdiction. Nearly all states exercise control over all surgical
procedures. However, the law is in an uncertain state of mind as to the
rights of a conceived but unborn fetus. Some legislatures have simply
defined a conceived but unborn child as a life in being. Courts have
struggled with the ethical, moral, and religious problems of a woman's
refusal to carry an embryo or fetus to term.

The word *abortion* is not mentioned in the United States Constitution. However, the fact that a right is not mentioned does not mean
that it doesn't exist. Some matters are properly read into the Constitution by judicial decree. The highest United States court says that
certain unstated things emanate from the Constitution. "Without
those peripheral rights the specific would be less secure ... specific
guarantees in the Bill of Rights have penumbras, formed by emana-
tions from these guarantees that help give them life and substance."
(*Griswold* v. *Connecticut* 381 U.S. 479, 455 [1965].) To be so protected
the liberty should be rooted in the traditions and conscience of the
people so as to be ranked as fundamental.

The right of privacy developed as such a peripheral right. The
most quoted recognition by the Supreme Court of the right of privacy credits the framers of the Constitution as having "conferred, as
against the government, the right to be left alone — the most comprehensive of rights and the right most valued by civilized man. To
protect that right, every unjustifiable intrusion by the government
upon the privacy of the individual, whatever means employed, must
be deemed a violation of the Fourth Amendment." (277 U.S. 438 at p.
478.)

By 1973 the Supreme Court was talking about the right of privacy
as having application in marriage, procreation, family relationships,

and in some abortions. By judicial legislation these judges have ruled that the traditions and consciences of our people are such that a woman has a Constitutional right to have an abortion until "the point at which a fetus is potentially able to live outside the mother's womb, albeit with artificial aid, and presumably capable of meaningful life outside the mother's womb." (*Roe* v. *Wade* 410 U.S. 113 [1973].)

In succeeding rulings the Court has said that a state may not require the consent of a spouse, or parental consent of a minor girl, as a condition for abortion during the first twelve weeks of pregnancy. It has also said that a state may not require a physician to preserve the life and health of a fetus prior to its ability to survive independently. All of this social policy is imposed upon us under the guise of the right of privacy. Even now, debate continues as to whether there is an independent constitutional right of privacy, and if such does exist, what it is.

The First Presidency of The Church of Jesus Christ of Latter-day Saints issued the following statement on January 27, 1973, in the *Church News* section of the *Deseret News,* page 7.

> In view of a recent decision of the United States Supreme Court, we feel it necessary to restate the position of the church on abortion in order that there be no misunderstanding of our attitude.
>
> The church opposes abortion and counsels its members not to submit to or perform an abortion except in the rare cases where, in the opinion of competent medical counsel, the life or good health of the mother is seriously endangered or where the pregnancy was caused by rape and produces serious emotional trauma in the mother. Even then it should be done only after counseling with the local presiding priesthood authority and after receiving divine confirmation through prayer.
>
> Abortion must be considered one of the most revolting and sinful practices in this day, when we are witnessing the frightening evidence of permissiveness leading to sexual immorality.
>
> Members of the church guilty of being parties to the sin of abortion must be subjected to the disciplinary action of the councils of the church as circumstances warrant. In dealing with this serious matter, it would be well to keep in mind the word of the Lord stated in the 59th Section of the Doctrine and Covenants, verse 6, "Thou shalt not steal; neither commit adultery, nor kill, nor do anything like unto it."
>
> As to the amenability of the sin of abortion to the laws of repentance and forgiveness, we quote the following statement

made by President David O. McKay and his counselors, Stephen L Richards and J. Reuben Clark, Jr., which continues to represent the attitude and position of the church:

"As the matter stands today, no definite statement has been made by the Lord one way or another regarding the crime of abortion. So far as is known, He has not listed it alongside the crime of the unpardonable sin and shedding of innocent human blood. That He has not done so would suggest that it is not in that class of crime and therefore that it will be amenable to the laws of repentance and forgiveness."

This quoted statement, however, should not, in any sense, be construed to minimize the seriousness of this revolting sin.

Church policy views most voluntarily induced abortions as "revolting and sinful practices." If a nonmember has committed such a sin and subsequently repents and petitions for baptism, she must have special interviews with the stake or mission president to determine worthiness. If members "submit to or perform an abortion except in rare cases" they are handled as transgressors. (See *General Handbook of Instructions*, number 21, page 45; see also *General Handbook Supplement* 1, item 14.) Repentance is possible for both nonmembers and members.

If a fetus is born dead, it is said to be *stillborn*, but the question of precisely when the spirit enters the body has not been answered. If a fertilized egg is independent life in being, having become a living soul as the home of a previously existing spirit, then the wanton and unjustified destruction of that mortal home presumably is an offense similar to murder. However, if the spirit does not enter the body until birth, then the wrongful destruction of the fetus prior to birth could be another and lesser offense. There is no authoritative Church position on this question, since the revelations do not specify the time when the spirit enters the body.

Some students have speculated that the spirit enters the body of the child at birth. By way of scriptural argument they point to "the voice of the Lord" coming to Nephi saying, "On the morrow come I into the world." (3 Nephi 1:12-13.) The Savior's earthly body obviously was in Mary's womb at the time of this conversation. However, the Lord's birth and mission were an exceptional case. More gospel students believe that the eternal spirit enters the body at some time prior to a child's birth. Brigham Young is quoted approvingly by President Joseph Fielding Smith and Elder Bruce R. McConkie as saying, "When the mother feels life come to her infant, it is the spirit entering the body preparatory to the immortal existence." (*Journal of Discourses* 17:143; Joseph Fielding Smith, *Doctrines of Salvation*, 2:280.) President Joseph Fielding Smith said, "Stillborn children should not be reported nor recorded as births and deaths on the records of the Church, but it is suggested that parents record in their own family records a name for each such stillborn child." (Joseph Fielding Smith, *Doctrines of Salvation*, 2:280; see also Bruce R. McConkie, *Mormon Doctrine*, page 768.)

A statement of the First Presidency appears to support the concept that the spirit enters the body prior to birth. It states: "The body of man enters upon its career as a tiny germ or embryo, which becomes an infant, quickened at a certain stage by the spirit whose tabernacle it is, and the child, after being born, develops into a man." (James R. Clark, *Messages of the First Presidency*, 4:205.)

This doctrine is a very comforting concept to mothers who have felt life within them and then have a stillbirth. Brigham Young stated: "Whether the spirit remains in the body [i.e. in its own body] a minute, an hour, a day, a year, or lives there until the body has reached a good old age," makes no difference in the resurrection. (See Joseph Fielding Smith, *Doctrines of Salvation*, 2:280-81.) President Smith gives it as his opinion that we should have hope "that *these little ones will receive a resurrection and then belong to us.*" (Joseph Fielding Smith, *Doctrines of Salvation*, 2:280.)

Masturbation

We address now a matter on which we disagree with the world as regards the significance of the practice.

Masturbation is the stimulation of the genital organs for sexual excitement. Most youth, particularly young men, come in contact with masturbation either in reality or in discussion.

Many would-be authorities today claim that the practice is natural and acceptable. The Church does not accept the world's sex norms. It has a higher norm. It is opposed to masturbation. The President of the Church has said: "Prophets anciently and today condemn masturbation. It induces feelings of guilt and shame. It is detrimental to spirituality. It indicates slavery to the flesh, not that mastery of it and the growth toward godhood which is the object of our mortal life. . . . No young man should be called on a mission who is not free from this practice." (Spencer W. Kimball, *The Miracle of Forgiveness* [Bookcraft, Inc., 1969], page 77.)

While masturbation is a sin, it is not to be considered in the same category as the other sexual sins discussed in this chapter. It is a weakness and it does require repentance. But repentance from this activity fortunately is relatively easy. One ceases the activity and lives the Christian law of self-control. This usually requires a greater effort at spirituality and an elevating of one's self-image.

My experience in counseling has demonstrated to me that this practice can bring many problems. I have seen young missionaries in the field lose the Spirit because of this weakness. By failing to overcome this temptation they recognize that they are not their own masters. While enslaved to this practice they cannot enjoy the fruits of the Spirit. In this respect it tends to spoil their missions. As they overcome it, they find a much greater satisfaction in themselves and enjoy the companionship of the Holy Ghost.

I have often reflected that such a seemingly small sin can cause consequences of much greater magnitude. Practiced with another person of the same sex it sometimes leads to the grievous sin of homosexuality. Certainly the practice, individually or with another, can delay a normal marriage, and within a marriage it can disrupt normal marital relations.

We must remember too that the thought is father of the act. Those who engage in this activity often conjure up images in their minds, fantasizing that they are committing sexual acts with those of the opposite sex. Some have told me they simultaneously looked at pornographic pictures. Quite obviously, while this is wrong in itself, it is a step toward tragic transgressions.

One of the great purposes of this earth life is to overcome the flesh. If a person does less than that he is not fulfilling the purpose of his creation.

Fornication

We come now to a sin of which younger family members must particularly beware, particularly in the modern climate of permissiveness. Parents need specially to instruct their youth on this subject.

Every normal person has planted into his or her physical being sexual appetites and desires. One of the purposes of the mortal probation is to see whether women and men will control their normal passions and use and enjoy them as God has commanded. The Lord set the proper control by these commandments: "Be fruitful, and multiply, and replenish the earth" (Genesis 1:28); "Thou shalt not commit adultery" (Exodus 20:14); and, "Ye should abstain from fornication." (1 Thessalonians 4:3.) Sexual union in marriage is proper and good. When participated in with the right intent it is honorable and a legitimate way to attain and sustain a loving oneness in marriage. Without the bonds of marriage, however, sexual indulgence is a debasing sin, abominable in the sight of Deity.

Fornication is sexual intercourse on the part of an unmarried person. It is a gross type of sexual immorality, and we are under commandment to abstain from it. (See 1 Thessalonians 4:3.) Unrepentant fornicators will not inherit the kingdom of God. (See 1 Corinthians 6:9-11.) The Saints are "not to company with fornicators." (1 Corinthians 5:9-13.) The Lord's answer to the devil's advocacy of fornication is, "Be chaste."

Adultery

Indulgence in fornication by a family member can bring traumatic effects on every other member. Even so, the effects of adultery in the family are even worse, since they involve one of the married partners, one of the parents. Quite apart from the offender, the effects on the spouse and the children can be literally devastating.

Adultery is the voluntary sexual intercourse between a married person and someone other than his or her legal spouse. All of the divine disapproval given fornication applies to adultery. In addition, adultery carries with it the breach of the marriage covenant, and thus is worse even than fornication.

The Lord God set the basis for all Western law in the Ten Commandments. One of these basic ten rules to govern society was, "Thou shalt not commit adultery." (Exodus 20:14.) It is so fundamental to the existence of an ordered society that the prophets have ranked adultery as second only to murder in the category of personal crimes. As a sexual sin of great enormity, it is "most abominable above all sins save it be the shedding of innocent blood or denying the Holy Ghost." (Alma 39:5.) In the days of Moses the penalty therefore was death: "the adulterer and the adulteress shall surely be put to death." (Leviticus 20:10.)

> In the initial day of judgment, at the Second Coming of our Lord, Christ "will be a swift witness . . . against the adulterers," and they shall be burned as stubble. (Malachi 3:5; 4:1.) Adulterers shall be cast down to hell; . . . and their eventual destiny — after suffering the torments of the damned until the second resurrection — shall be that of the telestial kingdom. (D&C 76:103-106.)

They shall not inherit the kingdom of God. (1 Corinthians
6:9-11.) [Bruce R. McConkie, *Mormon Doctrine*, pages 23-24.]

Adultery receives these ringing condemnations because it
"opens the flood gates of wickedness in general." (Bruce R. McConkie, *Mormon Doctrine*, page 24.) It is an attack on the family and
society. Divorce, illegitimacy, personal shame, and a host of social
problems and evils attend adulterous acts. Physical disease is often a
companion. And, more importantly, spiritual disease accompanies
such activity so as "to hinder [the actors] in recognizing and accepting
the gospel truths and thus becoming heirs of salvation." (Bruce R.
McConkie, *Mormon Doctrine*, page 24.) It is a sin that destroys the
fabric of society here and causes its participants to lose hope of salvation hereafter because they are not obeying celestial requirements.
There could hardly be a more destructive action.

"Adulterous acts are born spiritually before they are committed
temporally; they proceed out of the heart. (Matthew 15:19.) As a man
'thinketh in his heart, so is he.' (Proverbs 23:7.) Therefore,
'whosoever looketh on a woman to lust after her hath committed
adultery with her already in his heart.' (Matthew 5:27-28.)" (Bruce R.
McConkie, *Mormon Doctrine*, page 24.) This means that one who
wants to commit adultery with another, to the point of lusting after
that person, and would commit the act if given the opportunity, has
committed the sin in the heart. The Lord forecast the spiritual results
of this. "He that looketh on a woman to lust after her, or if any shall
commit adultery in their hearts, they shall not have the Spirit, but
shall deny the faith and shall fear." (D&C 63:16.)

Although it is always preferable not to have sinned in the first
place, in nearly all cases it is possible to repent of adultery and gain
forgiveness and be saved in the celestial kingdom of God. Those who
wholeheartedly repent and then conform to the Lord's law shall be
saved. (See 1 Corinthians 6:9-11.) "But he that has committed adultery and repents with all his heart, and forsaketh it, and doeth it no
more, thou shalt forgive." (D&C 42:25.)

But it appears that some people advance in righteousness, light
and faith to the point where, if they should commit such a great
offense, they could not fully repent of it. I was talking to the late
President Joseph Fielding Smith at one time about sins that were so
gross as to be considered unforgivable. As sins of this type he enum-
erated "the sin against the Holy Ghost; murder; and adultery under
some circumstances." I questioned him about the last-mentioned. As
an example, he indicated that he had felt he had reached a point of

sufficient understanding and knowledge that if he were to commit that sin he could not be fully forgiven.

I pressed the point by asking, "What about me? I'm a believer, with a testimony of the truthfulness of the gospel, and I have received the temple endowment." His reply was, "I don't know whether you know enough."

Thus forgiveness, with resultant celestial salvation, may well depend upon the light and knowledge enjoyed by the one guilty of the sin at the time of the act. Except for those whose calling and election has been made sure, full repentance for adultery is always possible.

This reassurance, however, is for the benefit of any who may have transgressed. It should not be construed as in any way minimizing the seriousness of the offense or the anguish and heartbreak the offender must suffer before forgiveness can be assured. If anyone were even contemplating this sin, from however remote a position, he would be best advised to read *The Miracle of Forgiveness*, by President Spencer W. Kimball, wherein the sorrow and suffering of the road back are faithfully portrayed.

Those who would gloss over this type of sexual immorality as merely actions within the concern of consenting adults and not within the scope of governmental sanctions, strike at the heart of the home and society. They either don't know of the mischief such advocacy would bring, or, knowing, are opposed to existing social and political institutions and are attempting to destroy them.

Homosexuality

In the realm of sexual sin there is yet another desire and practice which has grave implications for the perpetuation and unity of the family. I refer to homosexuality.

The exhibiting of sexual desires toward the members of one's own sex is called homosexuality. Female homosexuals are called lesbians.

Homosexuality has many forms. It may be only a mental state without outward behavior, or it may include complete emotional and sexual involvement with a member of the same sex. Thus there are two parts to homosexual behavior: the physical-sexual conduct and the emotional attachment.

Different degrees of homosexuality range from childhood experimentation to adult obsession. Some include serious emotional disturbance of which sexual misbehavior is often a symptom. Some include a conscious choice of a homosexual lifestyle; other degrees include those who have suffered traumatic experiences with resulting emotional scars. A traditional explanation for homosexuality is that a child has a domineering mother and a passive father.

Usually homosexuals may be classified in one of three broad categories: (1) those who are fully involved and engaged in forms of sexual activity, (2) those who think about homosexuality without being sexually involved, and (3) those in various stages between these extremes. Note that some people have made themselves bisexual and may engage in sexual activity with members of both sexes.

The First Presidency published the following statement.

> A homosexual relationship is viewed by The Church of Jesus Christ of Latter-day Saints as sin in the same degree as adultery and fornication.
>
> In summarizing the intended destiny of man, the Lord has declared: "For behold, this is my work and my glory — to bring to pass the immortality and eternal life of man." (Moses 1:39.) Eternal life means returning to the Lord's exalted presence and enjoying the privilege of eternal increase. According to his revealed word, the only acceptable sexual relationship occurs within the family between a husband and a wife.
>
> Homosexuality in men and women runs counter to these divine objectives and, therefore, is to be avoided and forsaken. Church members involved to any degree must repent. "By this ye may know if a man repenteth of his sins — behold, he will confess them and forsake them." (D&C 58:43.) Failure to work closely with one's bishop or stake president in cases involving homosexual behavior will require prompt Church court action. (*The Priesthood Bulletin,* February 1973 [volume 9, number 1], pages 2-3.)

Homosexuality is sin and as such has been condemned by ancient and modern prophets. (See Deuteronomy 23:17; Leviticus 20:13, 18:22; Romans 1:24-27; 1 Corinthians 6:9.) President Spencer W. Kimball has said, "The seriousness of the sin of homosexuality is equal to or greater than that of fornication or adultery." (Spencer W. Kimball, *The Miracle of Forgiveness,* pages 81-82.)

There are several reasons why homosexuality is both antisocial behavior and sinful. It violates the Lord's eternal plan for men and women's progress and deprives God's children of true happiness and genuine fulfillment in family life. It is in fact destructive of society's basic unit, the family. It is "carnal, sensual, and devilish" and has been declared as sinful as adultery and fornication. It debases and demeans the participants and may involve violent, criminal behavior.

There is no easy or even commonly accepted care for the homosexual. Professionally trained persons differ in their opinions regarding both the cause and the care. "There are those who tell you there is no cure and thus weaken your resolves and add to your frustrations. They *can* be cured. They *can* be eventually forgiven. Your problem *can* be solved." (Spencer W. Kimball, *New Horizons for Homosexuals* [pamphlet, 1971], page 5.)

Since emotional disorder is involved, repentance requires great resolve. But those who maintain improper behavior are often skilled at rationalization, and this seems to be particularly true with homosexuals. Their rationalization is that they were born that way. However, they answer their own contention in this regard. The "gay" movement itself, by urging complete freedom of sexual preference, is tacitly acknowledging that homosexuality is voluntarily chosen. In point of fact, "God did not make men [or women] evil. He did not make people 'that way.' " (Spencer W. Kimball, *New Horizons*, page 33.) To believe that immoral behavior is inborn or hereditary is to deny that men and women have the agency to choose between sin and righteousness. God has given us our "agency . . . that every man may be accountable for his own sins in the day of judgment." (D&C 101:78.) Our Lord's brother, James, put it succinctly: "Let no man say when he is tempted, I am tempted of God: for God cannot be tempted with evil, neither tempteth he any man: But every man is tempted, when he is drawn away of his own lust, and enticed." (James 1:13-14.) As with other transgressions, these types of abominations are learned behavior. The law of the gospel is that "all things which are good cometh of God; and that which is evil cometh of the devil." (Moroni 7:12.)

Western law prohibits many specific homosexual acts and outlaws other such acts under nuisance laws as offending public decency.

Homosexuality has become a prominent women's issue because of the proposed Equal Rights Amendment to the United States Constitution. Since this amendment would stop the federal and state governments from discriminating on the basis of sex, many constitutional lawyers assume that such an amendment would affect laws on homosexuality. Marriage laws are restricted to men and women. If the Equal Rights Amendment passed, would such laws have to be modified so as not to discriminate on a sexual preference? That is, would it then be constitutional to say that women could not marry women?

Homosexuals have already gone to the judiciary when they have been discriminated against. School boards are reluctant to hire known homosexuals because they don't want such models placed before the students, or because of the problems coming from the soliciting of impressionable youngsters, or for other reasons. The "gay" liberationists claim that they have been denied equal protection of the law, which right is guaranteed by the Fourteenth Amendment. They also claim rights of association under the First Amendment.

The federal judiciary is divided in determining whether a state agency can discriminate against homosexuals. What in my judgment are the best reasoned cases hold that, "the equal protection clause was not intended to safeguard a group presenting a clear and present danger of violation of the criminal laws of a State . . . what otherwise might be an impermissible distinction becomes a permissible distinction." The court holds that there is "an appropriate governmental interest furthered by this different treatment." It is proper state policy not to allow recognition of a group where such recognition "is likely to incite and produce the violations of the state's sodomy statutes."

The court handled the right of association in a similar vein: "The members of Gay Lib . . . are forced to express within the law their beliefs and views of homosexuality. . . . But it is a far different thing to show a right under the First Amendment to receive official school recognition of Gay Lib with all of the associational conditions that are likely to result therefrom." (*Gay Lib v. University of Missouri*, 416 F. Supp. 1350 [1976], pages 1370-1371.)

I do not believe that homosexuals have a right not to be treated differently from others. Their unnatural affections do not rise to the level of Constitutional rights.

Expert witnesses in the foregoing case established to the court's satisfaction that homosexuality is clearly abnormal behavior; that there are potential or latent homosexuals, and that what happens to them from the standpoint of environment can help cause them to become or not to become overt homosexuals; that homosexuality is a compulsive type of behavior, and concerted effort should be made to cease such practices; that it is undesirable for homosexuals to counsel other homosexuals, "the sick and abnormal counseling others who are similarly ill and abnormal" (*Gay Lib v. University of Missouri*, pages 1358-59); and that, finally, the more the homosexuals get together, the more laws are broken.

I know of no activities that could be as accurately characterized as the devil's substitute for God-given desires and pleasures as those found in this deviate abomination.

President Spencer W. Kimball said in a general conference: "If all the people in the world were to accept homosexuality, . . . the practice would still be a deep, dark sin." ("The Foundations of Righteousness," *Ensign,* November 1977, page 6; see also *The Miracle of Forgiveness,* pages 77-89.)

Decriminalization of Illegal Sexual Behavior

Traditionally, illicit sexual activity has been a criminal offense as well as a sin. It has been considered an offense against society as well as an offense against God. Proposals have been made which would decriminalize all forms of sexual behavior between consenting adults, including fornication, adultery, prostitution, homosexuality, and other forms of deviate sexual behavior. The most extreme proposals would even decriminalize commercialized sex, such as procuring for prostitution. Another crime usually included in decriminalization proposals is abortion. There are other such proposals outside of the scope of this discussion.

We should not underestimate the importance of the proposals I have listed. The publicity and political power gathering behind various decriminalization proposals is impressive indeed; current lists of organizations include such prestigious groups as the National Council on Crime and Delinquency, the President's Crime Commission, and even the American Bar Association. We cannot help recalling the scriptural use of the term "church of the devil" (1 Nephi 14:10) to denote all organizations — whether political, philosophical, educational, or religious — which take men and women on a course that leads them away from God and his laws. The Savior summed it up by saying, "He that is not with me is against me; and he that gathereth not with me scattereth abroad." (Matthew 12:30.)

Criminal law revisions already adopted or under consideration leave no doubt that we are witnessing revolutionary changes in the function and content of criminal law. These changes will also bring about significant departures from the Judeo-Christian standards of morality. A Book of Mormon anti-Christ claimed that "whatsoever a man did was no crime." (Alma 30:17.) This is the ultimate in decriminalization.

The devil's advocates in decriminalization have adopted a cleverly deceptive battle cry. They say, "Do away with victimless crimes." This is deceptive because there is no such thing as a victimless crime. There is only the question of who the victim is. In the crime of rape the major victim obviously is the female. In sexual crimes between consenting adults the victims include the family unit — the basis of society itself. Society is involved as the victim. Our society makes massive expenditures to cure social diseases and to care for those they render sick, disabled, or needy. Does society have an interest in children born out of wedlock? Does society have an interest in homes that are torn asunder by illicit sexual activity? The answers to these questions are obviously yes. Clearly, the use of the term *victimless crime* is a devious propaganda technique.

Most important, since the family structure is the basic supportive institution in our society, society is the victim of these crimes because they pose a threat to the integrity of the family structure.

Decriminalization of illicit sexual activity is a serious matter. Criminal law has a standard-setting and -teaching function. There are many apparent examples of the enormous educative influences of the law. Law focuses our attention on a particular problem. It enacts solutions. It provides us with reasons for the solutions. Sometimes the law puts the mark of official finality on controversial social issues. Consider the legality of labor unions and the right to strike; or the progressive income tax; or the right to be free from racial discrimination in government, common carriers, and places of public accommodations, or the cases of statutory entitlement of Social Security and certain welfare benefits. With the establishment of laws in these areas our society not only changed the law but changed its mind. These matters of great political division and philosophic differences have become well accepted. In the light of these illustrations who could say that reshaping the thinking of members of society is not one major effect of the law?

The *repeal* of laws can similarly have a reshaping effect. When certain activities are classified as crimes, this is understood as a public declaration that the conduct is immoral, bad, unwise, and unacceptable for society and the individual. When an elected legislative body, or an activist court, removes a criminal penalty, many citizens will understand this repeal as an official judgment that the decriminalized behavior is not harmful to the individual or to society. Indeed, many individuals will choose to interpret decriminalization as a mark of public approval of the conduct in question.

Criminal law has an important function other than the protection of an identifiable victim. That function is to reinforce certain moral values and standards. The law should and does legislate morality. As a past president of the Utah State Senate, I can say I was motivated by the thought that a legislative body ought to be engaged in the business of implementing into our positive law God's own concept of things. It always seemed to me that those who contend that you cannot legislate morality know little about legislation and are concerned less about morality. As I look back over my experiences in the Utah House of Representatives and the Senate, it seems to me that we legislated hardly anything else.

The question is, Whose morality or values is the law to teach? Dallin H. Oaks, President of Brigham Young University, delivered an excellent lecture on the subject entitled "The Popular Myth of the Victimless Crime." He said:

> But whose morality or values is the law to teach? Here we meet an old controversy over the relationship between criminal law and the principles of morality or right and wrong.... My support belongs to those who argue that society has the right to "legislate against immorality" because without a "common morality," ... defined as the moral judgment of the "reasonable man," society would disintegrate....
>
> Today no thoughtful American would advocate using the criminal law to enforce that portion of the religious-moral law pertaining to religious belief or practice. But religious principles of right and wrong or good and evil in matters of individual behavior continue to wield an important moral influence on the content of the criminal law through their effect on the opinions and actions of individual citizens in the lawmaking process....
>
> "In matters of morality, the law-maker's function, ... was to enforce those ideas about right and wrong which are already accepted by the society for which he was legislating and which were necessary to preserve its integrity.... In so doing they were reflecting and changing the collective morality which was the substitute in a democratic society for any other authority outside of the law." [Here the speaker is quoting Edward H. Levi.]
>
> Whether finding its origin in religious belief, ethical system, or rational process, this "collective morality" is a legitimate source of criminal law in our society. By this means our criminal laws teach and compel the observance of standards of behavior not demonstrably related to harm to others or the survival of society but nevertheless important to our individual or collective well-beings....
>
> Most of our laws — particularly our criminal laws — are, in fact, an expression of what our lawmakers deem good for society. ("The Popular Myth of the Victimless Crime," *Commissioner's Lecture Series* [Brigham Young University Press, 1974], page 6.)

The law cannot successfully depart too far from the collective morality. The law will be ineffective if it attempts to criminalize conduct that is not condemned by collective morality. The law will be discredited if it attempts to decriminalize conduct condemned under collective morality.

In 1977 the county commissioners in Dade County, Florida, passed an ordinance making it unlawful to discriminate against homosexuals in employment. The majority of the people in Dade County regard homosexuality as immoral, degrading, degenerate, and a threat to society. In an initiative petition election the people voted out the ordinance by a two-to-one vote. If the positive law fails to support the collective morality, the law will not stand.

Sometimes the fabric of our society is held together by a gossamer thread. Every means should be employed to raise the standard of our collective morality.

Each of the topics discussed in this chapter represents a modern assault on the family. Satan and his agents are hard at work in this attack, and the LDS family is a prime target. Parents need to be constantly alert for signs of any weakness in their family fortifications. Even more important, they need to seek the easier course of prevention rather than cure by teaching and warning their children of the dangers and pitfalls.

And, mother in the Church, the initiative for this can as readily come from you as from your husband.

7

Women's Rights and Wrongs

During the term of President John F. Kennedy I was invited to the Oval Office in the White House. I was fascinated by the memorabilia on the anteroom walls, including a letter in the handwriting of John Adams to his wife Abigail. It was a touching plea for her to join him in the White House. The letter began, "My dearest friend."

Some years later I got an insight into what had seemed to me to be an unusual appellation in an endearing communication to a wife. My insight came when I read a published letter Abigail Adams had written to her husband when he was away from home participating in the 1776 councils that were framing our federal papers. She wrote:

> I long to hear that you have declared an independancy — and by the way in the new Code of Laws which I suppose it will be necessary for you to make I desire you would Remember the Ladies, and be more generous and favourable to them than your ancestors. . . . If perticuliar care and attention is not paid to the Ladies we are determined to foment a Rebelion, and will not hold ourselves bound by any Laws in which we have no voice, or Representation.
>
> That your Sex are Naturally Tyrannical is a Truth so thoroughly established as to admit of no dispute, but such of you

as wish to be happy willingly give up the harsh title of Master for the more tender and endearing one of Friend. (*The Feminist Papers,* ed. Alice S. Rossi [New York: Columbia University Press, 1973], pages 10-11.)

And so it was that a wise husband had addressed his wife as Friend.

In her now widely read "Remember the Ladies" letter, Abigail establishes herself as a cultured and refined Christian woman. She said: "Men of Sense in all Ages abhor those customs which treat us only as the vassals of your Sex. Regard us then as Beings placed by providence under your protection and in immitation of the Supreme Being make use of that power only for our happiness." (Alice S. Rossi, *The Feminist Papers,* page 11.)

The cause of women's rights would have been better served if other women concerned with this cause had done their championing within the bounds of the Judeo-Christian moral and ethical standards as did Abigail Adams.

A contemporary of Abigail Adams, Mary Wollstonecraft (1759-1797), is usually described as one of the early feminist activists. Her initial argument is sound. "[B]odily strength seems to give man a natural superiority over woman; and this is the only solid basis on which the superiority of the sex can be built." (From "A Vindication of the Rights of Woman," quoted in Alice S. Rossi, *The Feminist Papers,* page 54.) She makes a strong argument for individual education — male and female. Her healthy confidence that education is the key was a significant contribution to the cause of women's rights. However, she thought and acted outside the Judeo-Christian norms in terms of marriage and sexual disciplines. "I here throw down my gauntlet, and deny the existence of sexual virtues, not excepting modesty." (Alice S. Rossi, *The Feminist Papers,* page 63.) Her cause suffered by her loss of respectability.

Another illustration of a social "reformer" and feminist activist was Francis Wright (1795-1852). She established a social experiment in Tennessee called "Nashoba." Her notion was that women should not forfeit their individual rights or existence. She argued for a "blending of the white man and the black" and for a nonformal, nonmonogamous sexual union relationship. Americans called her experiment a "free love colony," and any serious contribution that she might have otherwise made was lost. Her movement ceased to exist. (See Alice S. Rossi, *The Feminist Papers,* pages 92-93.)

So also with the able early woman writer Harriet Martineau (1802-1876). She made some very astute sociological observations about the place of women in early America, such as: "Indulgence is given her as a substitute for justice." She said: "I am in truth very thankful for not having married at all. . . . My strong will . . . makes me fit only to live alone. . . . The older I have grown, the more serious and irremediable have seemed to me the evils and disadvantages of married life as it exists among us at this time." (From "Society in America," quoted in Alice S. Rossi, *The Feminist Papers,* pages 125, 121.)

Friedrich Engels and his friend Karl Marx seemed to influence the more radical early feminists. They made the attack on the family as an article of their faith. Marx: "The modern family contains in germ, not only slavery . . . , but also serfdom. . . . It contains *in miniature* all the contradictions which later extend throughout society and its state." Engels: "Monogamous marriage comes on the scene as the subjugation of the one sex by the other." (From "The Origin of the Family," quoted in Alice S. Rossi, *The Feminist Papers,* pages 480, 482.)

In 1869 John Stuart Mill published his noted work on women's rights, *The Subjection of Women.* The arguments he there delineated were, no doubt, discussed and honed to a cutting sharpness with his brilliant wife, Harriet Taylor Mill. He wrote:

> The object of this Essay is to explain as clearly as I am able, the grounds of an opinion which I have held . . . : That the principle which regulates the existing social relations between the two sexes — the legal subordination of one sex to the other — is wrong in itself, and now one of the chief hindrances to human improvement; and that it ought to be replaced by a principle of perfect equality, admitting no power or privilege on the one side, nor disability on the other. (From "The Subjection of Women," quoted in Alice S. Rossi, *The Feminist Papers,* page 196.)

Mill's "stature as an eminent Englishman . . . and his intellectual accomplishments [gave a] boost" to the woman's rights movement. His arguments are as valid today as when they were written. There is a constant relevancy for his "morality of justice." (Alice S. Rossi, *The Feminist Papers,* page 194.) He stood for "the equality of married persons before the law"; and he supported the "common arrangement [of the family], by which the man earns the income and the wife superintends the domestic expenditure." (Alice S. Rossi, *The Feminist Papers,* page 212.)

He argued for equal rights based on intellectual equality and made a plea for political equality. He provided the theoretical framework for many feminist causes: voting rights, status in politics, moral crusades and temperance movements, and domestic relations law.

Twenty years before Mill's great defense, "the first woman's rights meeting in American history took place in a Methodist church in Seneca Falls, New York, on July 19 and 20, 1848." A handful of women met who had prepared a Declaration of Sentiments a few days before. "The ninth was the demand, revolutionary for its time: 'Resolved, That it is the duty of the women of this country to secure to themselves the sacred right to the elective franchise." Women's suffrage was the first overriding women's issue. "The two central figures in the Seneca Falls drama were Elizabeth Cady Stanton [1815-1902] and Lucretia [Coffin] Mott [1789-1880]." (Alice S. Rossi, *The Feminist Papers*, page 241.)

In Nauvoo, Illinois, in April of 1842 the Prophet Joseph Smith met with the Female Relief Society, an organization of LDS women, and gave instructions on the rights and privileges of women in the Church. As recorded in his diary, he "gave a lecture on the Priesthood, showing how the sisters would come in possession of the privileges, blessings and gifts of the Priesthood, and that the signs should follow them." (Joseph Smith, *History of the Church*, 4:602.) In the meeting this man of God said: *"I now turn the key in your behalf in the name of the Lord, and this Society shall rejoice, and knowledge and intelligence shall flow down from this time henceforth; this is the beginning of better days to the poor and needy, who shall be made to rejoice and pour forth blessings on your heads."* (Joseph Smith, *History of the Church*, 4:607; italics added.)

Thus the time had come when the special talents of women would be recognized in the Church. Knowledge and intelligence was to be given them in their work in the Society. It is interesting to note that six years later the first women's rights meetings in America took place in Seneca Falls, New York, as referred to above.

The Latter-day Saint women were not only on the frontiers of western America, they were on the frontiers of women's organizations for justice, education, cultural refinement, and service. Joseph Smith said these women's knowledge might "extend to all the world." He cautioned, "Let your labors be mostly confined to those around you . . . your administering should be confined to the circle of your immediate acquaintance." (Joseph Smith, *History of the Church*, 4:607.)

In my research I have found no woman's organization now in existence that has had continuous existence as long as has the Relief Society of The Church of Jesus Christ of Latter-day Saints.

In 1852 Brigham Young said in a general conference: "Now, sisters, I want you to vote also, because women are the characters that rule the ballot box." (*Journal of Discourses*, 1:218.)

With their prophet turning the key in their behalf, and with succeeding Church leaders espousing women's right to vote, Mormon women were spared the century of struggle that other women in the United States had to make for this right. Mormon society gave its women the right to vote without any discernible demand for it among the women themselves.

Utah women voted in city and municipal elections before their sisters anywhere exercised their franchise, and Utah Territory enacted woman suffrage in February of 1870, just as it gave the men the right. Citizens were given the right to vote not because they were men or women, but because they were people. (See Eleanor Flexner, *Century of Struggle, The Woman's Rights Movement in the United States* [Cambridge: Harvard University Press, 1959], page 165.) Wyoming women were accorded the right to vote in the Wyoming Territory in 1869 and had the opportunity to vote in the elections of 1870 and 1871. The first four states to adopt woman suffrage were Wyoming, Colorado, Utah, and Idaho.

The right to vote was the overriding women's issue until the Nineteenth Amendment to the United States Constitution was adopted. From the Seneca Falls meeting and its resolution to secure the elective franchise for women came numerous local women's groups. The Puritan ethic provided much of the philosophic backdrop for the movements. (See Alan P. Grimes, *The Puritan Ethic and Woman Suffrage* [New York: Oxford University Press, 1967].) On the world scene the Protestant nations in general were the ones wherein women were successful in obtaining the vote.

During the summer of 1876 the United States was celebrating its centennial with a huge exposition in Philadelphia. The National Women Suffrage Association opened headquarters in Philadelphia. Susan Anthony — single, and therefore legally entitled to enter into a business contract — signed the lease. From this came the Women's Declaration of 1876. The fact that this declaration aroused little furor, as compared to the Declaration of Sentiments from Seneca Falls, showed that the climate of public opinion was changing.

In 1889 a new state was seeking admission to the Union. Wyoming asked for the privilege of being the first state to grant women political equality. Its proposed and adopted constitution contained provision for full woman suffrage. On July 10, 1890, Wyoming was admitted to the Union. Wyoming celebrated its newly won statehood in Cheyenne on July 23, 1890, the flag honoring the occasion being presented to the governor by the mother of woman suffrage in Wyoming, Mrs. Esther Morris.

In 1896, after six previous requests by the people of Utah Territory, Utah was admitted into the Union. Utah, also, had a complete woman's suffrage provision in its constitution when it was admitted.

The first proposal to amend the Constitution to provide for woman suffrage was offered by Senator Sargent of California in 1878, at the request of Miss Susan B. Anthony. The final amendment was declared adopted August 26, 1920. There were stormy, frustrating years of struggle in between.

In 1916 a National Woman's Party was organized. It campaigned in twelve states. The Woman's Party was generally an anti-Democratic Party and specifically opposed the Democratic incumbent president Woodrow Wilson. President Wilson was running against the Republican candidate, Charles Evans Hughes, on a record of reform. The President carried ten of the twelve "suffrage states."

President Wilson came to favor woman suffrage. He publicly stated he would make the journey from Washington, D.C., to his home in Princeton to vote in favor of a New Jersey referendum for women's suffrage in October of 1915. In January of 1918 President Wilson committed himself to leadership in favor of an amendment to the United States Constitution giving women the right to vote. With the presidential support, the amendment passed the House with the two-thirds majority necessary to pass a Constitutional amendment. It took another year and a half to get it through the Senate. President Wilson actively intervened by taking the sensational step of addressing the Senate on a measure it was then in the act of debating.

The states had to ratify the Nineteenth Amendment to give it effect. Utah ratified on September 30, the thirteenth state to do so, Wyoming, inexplicably, was the twenty-seventh state to ratify on January 25, 1920. The Amendment reads:

> Clause 1. The right of the citizens of the United States to vote shall not be denied or abridged by the United States or by any state on account of sex.
>
> Clause 2. Congress shall have power to enforce this article by appropriate legislation.

The courts have held that this amendment prohibits discrimination against women in the interpretation and administration of laws relating to suffrage qualifications and the conduct of elections. It is said to be self-executing, and by its own force and effect legally expunged the word *male* and the masculine pronoun from constitutions and laws defining voting qualifications. The right to vote now applies to both sexes.

The following is a computation of human effort made by Carrie Chapman Carr quoted in *Century of Struggle,* page 176. The revised edition was published in 1975 by the Harvard University Press in Cambridge, Massachusetts. This notable work is the best scholarship I have come across in tracing the rights of women in the United States. I quote from it:

> To get the word "male" in effect out of the Constitution cost the women of the country fifty-two years of pauseless campaign. . . . During that time they were forced to conduct fifty-six campaigns of referendum to make voters; 480 campaigns to get legislatures to submit suffrage amendments to voters; 47 campaigns to get state constitutional conventions to write woman suffrage into state constitutions; 277 campaigns to get state party conventions to include woman suffrage planks; 30 campaigns to get presidential party conventions to adopt woman suffrage planks in party platforms; and 19 campaigns with 19 successive Congresses.

So much of woman's history has been the history of their attempt to secure the vote that it has been said that feminism died with the passage of the suffrage amendment. At any rate, the great focus of women's movements in the last half of the nineteenth century and the first decades of the twentieth century successfully brought women into the mainstream of American politics by securing their use of the ballot box.

The inspired concept of self-determination — that we all might be accountable for our own actions — has the approbation of God. The Prophet Joseph Smith recorded this divine approval. "Therefore, it is not right that any man should be in bondage one to another. And for this purpose have I established the Constitution of this land, by the hands of wise men whom I raised up unto this very purpose, and redeemed the land by the shedding of blood." (D&C 101:79-80.)

The Saints have thus considered the Constitution an inspired document and prayed that the principles contained therein "be established forever." (D&C 109:54.) I personally feel that the Constitution expounded the concept of self-determination and "moral agency which [God gave]" (D&C 101:78) more after the Nineteenth Amendment than it did before.

Through the voting process women commenced to be selected to substantially every elective office. They have become, and are becoming, a proper part of the decision-making process and are executing and adjudging the laws.

I think it is now a generally accepted truth that, although men and women are not identical, they share equal rights. Every good thing in woman that craves expression and activity should have the freedom to reach for that expression. Barriers of discrimination and unequal treatment should be broken. This was the original aim of the women's rights movement.

Notwithstanding the great breakthrough in voting rights and political participation, many women seem to have been isolated and still seem lacking in real happiness. One of the aims of the movement was that woman was to be free to direct her own destiny. What happened to this worthy goal and the enthusiasm and effort it generated? Surely the concepts of "emancipation" were too narrowly construed and, in one important area, seriously misdirected.

This misdirection is shown in the fact that the passion many feminists have for equal rights includes a woman's right for sexual gratification. They view sex morals as inhibitory and repressive. As Margaret Sanger put it, they feel "no woman can call herself free who does not own and control her body." (Alice S. Rossi, *The Feminist Papers,* pages 520-21.) Their argument is that without the means to prevent and to control the timing of conception, economic and political rights have limited meaning for women.

Birth control before pregnancy and abortion after pregnancy have thus become a large part of the cry of the modern feminist. To the conservative forces of society, to those whose spiritual roots come from the Judeo-Christian ethic, or to those who have come to the women's movement through its Puritan, prohibition workings, such sexual morals are alien doctrine. Its protagonists are not viewed as worthy models. In the area of sex, the feminist movement reverted back to its earliest days — outside the accepted norms of society. The extremists, once again, challenged the institution of marriage and were not viewed as worthy models by the majority of people.

Clearly, women were united in their struggle for voting rights. Just as clearly, they were divided by this new sexual revolution. Judging from their use of the ballot box, by way of the several state legislatures, a very sizable majority of women who oppose abortion on demand, one of the mottos of the new sexualists, have let this opposition be felt.

Equal Rights Amendment

The women's rights movement of the late nineteenth and early twentieth centuries concentrated on obtaining the vote for women. Only the most radical persons called into question the assumption that woman's place was primarily in the home. In the 1970s there has been a demand for change. Equal rights advocates are insisting upon a broad reexamination of "woman's place." They operate on a very questionable assumption that as long as woman's place is defined as separate it will be defined as inferior. (Barbara Brown et al., "The Equal Rights Amendment," *Yale Law Review* 80 [April 1971] page 874.)

A proposed Twenty-seventh Amendment to the U.S. Constitution was first passed with a constitutional majority by the House of Representatives in 1970. It then died in the Senate. Subsequently it was passed by both legislative bodies and submitted to the states for ratification. It reads:

Equality of rights under the law shall not be denied or abridged by the United States or by any State on account of sex.

This has been the hallmark of the women's movement in the 1970s. At the time of this writing, this ratification procedure is continuing. The approval of three more states is necessary for ratification.

Fifteen states (Alaska, Colorado, Connecticut, Hawaii, Illinois, Maryland, Massachusetts, Montana, New Mexico, Pennsylvania, Texas, Utah, Virginia, Washington, and Wyoming) have in their constitutions provisions which are substantially identical to the proposed Equal Rights Amendment.

In its early pioneer days, Utah had started out with an equal rights provision in its constitution that was enacted without agitation by any special interest groups. It reflected the implementation of the religious principle of equality before God and the ideal of equality among mortal persons.

Although there is substantial unanimity among women's groups with reference to the various states' equal rights provisos, women are divided when it comes to the proposed Twenty-seventh Amendment to the Federal Constitution. Barbara B. Smith, general president of the Relief Society of The Church of Jesus Christ of Latter-day Saints, spoke as follows of the roles of men and women and of the Equal Rights Amendment:

The unique roles of men and women as delineated in the scriptures are clearly ones of love and caring for each other; they are mutually supportive and sharing — not one being superior or inferior, but with a balance of responsibilities. . . .

There are troubling issues of concern to women, and women desire that some of the wrongs of the past be corrected . . . such things as:

1. Unequal pay for equal work.
2. Unequal opportunity for promotions and advancements in paid employment; little voice in major public decision-making.
3. Guilt over failure to fit standardized or stereotyped roles.
4. Traditional deference to the concept of male supremacy.
5. Restrictions on the use of credit and credit cards.
6. The inability to obtain home loans and housing.
7. Discrimination against the administration of a child's estate.
8. Restrictive marital duties and parental obligations.
9. Restrictions on school entrance and activities.
10. Inequities in property rights, job benefits, and inheritance.

There are others. . . .

It is my considered judgment that *The Equal Rights Amendment is not the way.*

Passage of the amendment may nullify all laws concerning the gamut of domestic relations in such matters as financial liability of a father to support his wife and children, or the awarding of custody of children in divorce actions, which now provide favorable treatment for women.

It may be very distressing for women to find that the right of privacy as now provided in laws, rulings, and ordinances is no longer present. Military conscription of women may be interpreted to be a mandate of the act. They may find themselves "locked-into" a system which makes no allowance for the physical, biological, or emotional differences in the sexes. . . .

It seems unlikely that it [ERA] can accommodate for the fundamental differences and appropriate roles of men and women. Once it is passed, the enforcement will demand an undeviating approach which will create endless problems for an already troubled society. . . .

Is there a law which is unfair to women? If so, change it. . . . Make *sure* the uniqueness of the individual is protected and the family strengthened. . . .

Equal rights are not necessarily *women's rights* and, indeed, indiscriminately applied *equality may abolish women's rights.* (Barbara B. Smith, "Receive the Gift Bestowed," [address delivered at the Institute of Religion, University of Utah], December 13, 1974.)

Notwithstanding the apparently simple justice of the wording of the proposed amendment, many women do not believe that the Equal Rights Amendment is a continuation of the woman suffrage movement that gave so many women the right to vote.

Many feel that constitutional amendments should be viewed as political acts of last resort, and that if any other effective way can be found to cure a political illness the alternative should be tried first. This position makes ERA unnecessary.

Federal legislation is different from state legislation. With ERA passed, all control and application would come from federal authorities and not be subject to change or control by state legislatures or state authorities. This centralization is viewed with some alarm in the light of precedents coming from the federal establishment. The ERA effectively preempts lawmakers in individual states from enacting laws making any distinction between men and women, however reasonable such distinction might be. If passed, it would change domestic relations laws from traditional state enactment and control to that of the federal judiciary.

No one is certain how far the application of ERA would go. An eminent constitutional law professor from the Harvard Law School, Paul A. Freund, gives this apt analogy. "The choice resembles that in medicine between a single broad-spectrum drug with uncertain and unwanted side effects and a selection of specific pills for specific ills." (Quoted in an unpublished address by Rex E. Lee, Dean of J. Reuben Clark School of Law, Brigham Young University, "Thoughts Concerning the Equal Rights Amendment.")

Many, including those who support ERA, agree that ERA would require women as well as men to be subject to military draft and that in times of war it would require women to be used in combat zones. (See *Yale Law Review,* 80:871, 908, 948.)

A technical application of the proposed amendment would require, among other things, integration of state college dormitories and public restrooms. The proponents of ERA admit this but say that the established legal doctrine of privacy might well keep the courts from such a strict construction of the amendment. The privacy concept, however, is based, for the most part, on case law. It is an unclear concept at best, and in the face of a Constitutional amendment might be rejected or found not applicable.

In the event that ERA is ratified, women stand to lose many present statutory entitlements. Domestic relations laws are replete with statutory advantages in favor of women. For instance, many states provide that an act of marriage bestows a one-third interest in her husband's real property upon the wife and that a married man cannot sell his property without his wife's signature. However, a married woman can freely sell her property without her husband's signature; the marriage gives the husband no interest in his wife's property. Under ERA, men may not be legally responsible for the support of their wives. Another loss would be registered in areas of protective legislation which discriminates in favor of women in hazardous employment, such as in restricting what they can be required to lift.

ERA could go beyond even the desires of its proponents. They claim it affects only "state actions"; but that terminology has been so broadly construed by the federal judiciary that ERA well might extend into private activity and commence a controlling of individual and family relationships. Its proponents proclaim that the proposed amendment's "rights" include all forms of privileges, immunities, benefits, and responsibilities.

Elder Neal A. Maxwell of the Presidency of the First Quorum of the Seventy told a citizens' organization in Florida in March of 1977, "ERA is not the answer — indeed, it would become the problem." He continued:

> One of the great challenges of the ERA is that it will produce undesired, uncertain, unintended, unforeseen, and unwanted consequences — despite all the assurances that may be given in this regard. There is no reason to presume that we are bright enough to foresee all the consequences that will follow from the amendment if it were passed.
>
> Our inability to measure consequences is one of the reasons for not passing the ERA. . . . There are already contradictory expectations concerning what will happen if ERA is passed. . . . Some ERA supporters are unisex and anti-family — will their intent prevail? Would ERA confer upon homosexuals privileges or status not intended? . . . What will the impact of the ERA be upon the institution of the family? No one really knows. . . . The family garden is still the best place to grow happy humans. The passage of the ERA will damage and disrupt the family garden. . . .

In attempting to remedy one form of deprivation by encouraging even more women to leave the home, the ERA may create other deprivations that are even more serious, he said.

> The Equal Rights Amendment is also undesirable because it would deprive lawmakers and government officials of the right to make laws and regulations to honor vital differences in the

roles of men and women, especially in respect to the family. . . . Our homes are the headwaters of our civilization. If we poison the stream at its source, it doesn't matter how many remedial filtration plants we have downstream, there will be inevitable and perhaps irreversible damage. ("LDS Official Attacks ERA," *Deseret News,* 24 March 1977, pages B-1, B-16.)

The First Presidency issued the following statement:

From its beginnings, The Church of Jesus Christ of Latter-day Saints has affirmed the exalted role of woman in our society.

In 1842, when women's organizations were little known, the Prophet Joseph Smith established the women's organization of the Church, the Relief Society, as a companion body of the priesthood. The Relief Society continues to function today as a vibrant, worldwide organization aimed at strengthening motherhood and broadening women's learning and involvement in religious, compassionate, cultural, educational, and community pursuits.

In Utah, where our Church is headquartered, women received the right to vote in 1870, fifty years before the Nineteenth Amendment to the Constitution granted the right nationally. There have been injustices to women before the law and in society generally. These we deplore.

There are additional rights to which women are entitled. However, we firmly believe that the Equal Rights Amendment is not the answer.

While the motives of its supporters may be praiseworthy, ERA as a blanket attempt to help women could indeed bring them far more restraints and repressions. We fear it will even stifle many God-given feminine instincts.

It would strike at the family, humankind's basic institution. ERA would bring ambiguity and possibly invite extensive litigation.

Passage of ERA, some legal authorities contend, could nullify many accumulated benefits to women in present statutes.

We recognize men and women as equally important before the Lord, but with differences biologically, emotionally, and in other ways.

ERA, we believe, does not recognize these differences. There are better means for giving women, and men, the rights they deserve. (*Ensign,* December 1976, page 79.)

8

Equality

What does it mean to be equal? To be equal, persons need not be identical. They need not be the same size, for instance. Persons are said to be equal if they have broadly the same abilities, enjoy similar rights, or are alike in quality.

Women and men may be equal in the basic attributes of godliness. That is, they may be alike in knowledge, in justice, in judgment, in mercy, and in faith. They may be equal in love for God and man.

Women and men may be equal in spirituality, although "all have not every gift given unto them." (D&C 46:11.) Some are given "to know that Jesus Christ is the Son of God.... To others it is given to believe on their words...to know the differences of administration...the diversities of operation.... To some is given the word of wisdom,...knowledge,...faith to be healed;...faith to heal,...the working of miracles,...prophecy, discerning of spirits,... tongues,...the interpretation of tongues...and unto the bishop...to discern. (D&C 46:13-25, 27.)

Women and men may be equal in good works.

Women and men may be equal in intellectuality.

Women and men may be equal in the possession of talents.

Women and men may be equal under the law. Their votes may be counted alike. In the United States the basic federal papers hold "that all men are created equal; that they are endowed by their Creator with certain unalienable rights." (The Declaration of Independence.) But civil equality does not mean that all persons are created with the same talents and abilities. Some are more quick to perceive than others. Some are stronger in body. Civil equality does not mean sameness in personal attributes and characteristics. Thus men and women may be equal in rights without being the same. Moreover, the fact that they fill differing roles does not make them unequal in the sense of worth.

As we have discussed before, there are some things wherein men may not be the equal of women. They are not equal in the ability to conceive and bear children; they do not have "mother love" and its special attibutes. Perhaps men are not equal in some aspects of compassion or tenderheartedness.

There are some areas wherein women may not be the equal of men. For instance, they are not equal in physical strength and size. They are not equal in certain prerogatives of leadership in the home and the Church. In this aspect consider the Creation as described in Moses 3. Note how the Lord figuratively and by directive helps to define Adam's and Eve's roles. Does the symbolism help to teach us anything? For instance, how is man shown to be the protector?

Numerous scriptures, especially in Genesis and the writings of Paul, dwell on the relationship and status of wife and husband in terms which the "liberated" woman of today finds unacceptable, even offensive. I refer particularly to such expressions as "thy desire shall be to thy husband, and he shall rule over thee" (Genesis 3:16); "Wives, submit yourselves unto your own husbands" (Colossians 3:18); "and the wife see that she reverence her husband" (Ephesians 5:33). Actually, the reason for objection is a lack of understanding. Awareness and willing acceptance of God's plans and purposes for all his children of both sexes would remove all disagreement.

Without the understanding that comes from modern revelations, and lacking the inspiration of the Spirit of God, some feminists simply reject the Bible. "Feminist philosophies and theologians strongly reject the notion that the Bible, which has been so blatantly shorn of female imagery, should be considered the word of God." (Marilyn Warenski, *Patriarchs and Politics, The Plight of The Mormon Woman* [McGraw-Hill Book Co., 1978], page 260.) This leads the feminists to a direct confrontation with the religion that the Bible espouses. "Feminism suffers from a lack of precise definition. However it may be defined, the point must be emphasized again that feminism can never properly be perceived as compatible with patriarchal religion." (Marilyn Warenski, *Patriarchs and Politics,* page 223.) I believe that a Christian woman must cope with the concepts clearly communicated in the Bible. Members of the Church "believe the Bible to be the word of God as far as it is translated correctly." (Articles of Faith 1:8.)

With the restoration of the gospel, the revealed word of God, new light has flooded this area of concern as well as many others. As an example I quote some of Paul's words to the Ephesians, placed in the proper context of the mutual responsibilities of husband and wife together with the commentary a modern apostle makes upon them. And I submit that anyone who reads this prayerfully and with a mind and heart open to truth will acknowledge its inspired wisdom.

Wives, submit yourselves unto your own husbands, as unto the Lord.

For the husband is the head of the wife, even as Christ is the head of the church: and he is the saviour of the body.

Therefore as the church is subject unto Christ, so let the wives be to their own husbands in every thing.

Husbands, love your wives, even as Christ also loved the church, and gave himself for it;

That he might sanctify and cleanse it with the washing of water by the word.

That he might present it to himself a glorious church, not having spot, or wrinkle, or any such thing; but that it should be holy and without blemish.

So ought men to love their wives as their own bodies. He that loveth his wife loveth himself.

For no man ever yet hated his own flesh! but nourisheth and cherisheth it, even as the Lord the church:

For we are members of his body, of his flesh, and of his bones.

For this cause shall a man leave his father and mother, and shall be joined unto his wife, and they two shall be one flesh.

This is a great mystery: but I speak concerning Christ and the church.

Nevertheless let every one of you in particular so love his wife even as himself; and the wife see that she reverence her husband. (Ephesians 5:22-33.)

Marriage and love are eternal. Those who continue in the married state in eternity have exaltation and possess the attributes of godliness. They then love each other with a perfect and abiding love. And the marriage status, here in mortality, is the schooling, preparatory state in which love may grow and blossom into that fulness of joy and perfection which can come only when body and spirit are inseparably connected with immortality. (D&C 93:33-34.)

Hence, Paul, using Christ as his pattern, here teaches: Christ has taken the Church as his bride; he is married to that body of true believers who have become saints; they are "members of his body, of his flesh, and of his bones." He loves them, gave himself for them, and cleansed and sanctified them; he will perfect and glorify them so they shall dwell with him eternally in holiness and exaltation. He is their Savior.

And so it is in the true order of matrimony. A man marries a wife "for time and for all eternity" (D&C 132:18); those so married are separate from all others; she is now his, he is hers, and they become one flesh; they are no longer twain but have one body. Those who receive "all the ordinances of the house of the Lord," must get them "in the same way that Jesus Christ obtained" them (*Teachings,* p. 308), thus following the pattern of Christ their Head. They must then love their wives, sacrifice for their well-being and salvation, and guide them in holiness until they are cleansed, sanctified, and perfected, until they are prepared for exaltation in that glorious heaven where the family unit continues. Husbands thus become in effect the saviors of their wives (and their families!), and these in turn are called to bestow reverence and respect upon the heads of their eternal family units. Truly, in Paul's language, "This is a great mystery," at least until men's minds are opened by the power of the Spirit.

In the patriarchal order of celestial marriage, the husband is the eternal and everlasting head of the wife; he is the Lord's agent and representative, holding the fulness of the holy Melchizedek Priesthood; accordingly, he is the proper recipient of respect from his eternal companion, "Even as Sara obeyed Abraham, calling him lord." (1 Pet. 3:6.) And Abraham — acting in the true spirit of Christ, and setting the pattern for all who should thereafter enter into that same order of enduring matrimony — showered like appreciation and respect upon Sarah.

Marriage is a partnership, but there is a senior partner. God set man to lead, to preside, to be the last word. Woman is obligated to conform, to obey, to be in subjection to the will of the husband, as long as his rulership is exercised in righteousness. (Bruce R. McConkie, *Doctrinal New Testament Commentary,* 3 volumes [Bookcraft, Inc., 1970], 2:518-19.)

Everlasting to Everlasting

God is "from everlasting to everlasting" (D&C 20:17), and men and women were with him "before the world was made." (D&C

49:17.) To understand the justice of Christian disciplines and the assignment of roles in the flesh one must understand that we existed as
conscious identities before this mortal life and that we will continue to
exist as conscious identities after this mortal existence. We are in the
second act of a three-act play. If we were to be associated with this
world only, then there would be no justice and no reason for being.
To understand equality one must first understand immortality.

We have previously referred to the first act in the play, our premortal existence. President Joseph F. Smith, sixth president of the
Church and eminent doctrinarian, has added to our knowledge about
activities in the world of spirits after mortal death. He related the
following in a funeral sermon for Mary A. Freeze.

> While the brethren and sisters were speaking, the thought
> naturally passed through my mind — what will be her occupa-
> tion in the world to come? What will she be doing there? We are
> told that she will not be idle. She could not be idle. In God's
> plans, there is no such thing as idleness. God is not pleased with
> the thought of idleness. He is not idle, and there is no such thing
> as inertia in the providences and in the purposes of God. We are
> either growing and advancing, or are retrograding. We are not
> stationary. We must grow. The principles of everlasting growth
> and development tend to glory, to exaltation, to happiness, and
> to a fulness of joy. What has she been doing? She has been work-
> ing in the temple, among other things. She has been work-
> ing, also, as a minister of life among young women of The
> Church of Jesus Christ of Latter-day Saints. She has labored
> diligently and earnestly in trying to persuade the daughters of
> Zion to come to a knowledge of the truth as she possessed it. She
> seemed to be thoroughly established in it. I have never discov-
> ered the least symptom of any dubiety in her mind in reference
> to the gospel of Jesus Christ. She has been laboring to bring
> others of the daughters of Zion to the same standard of knowl-
> edge, faith and understanding of the principles of the gospel of
> Christ that she herself possessed, a ministering angel and a
> mother in Israel, seeking the salvation of other daughters and
> other mothers in Israel. What can you conceive of grander than a
> calling like that? Then, as I said, she has been at work in the
> temple. What for? Administering ordinances that God has re-
> vealed are essential to the salvation of the living and their prep-
> aration for greater exaltation and glory here and hereafter, and
> also for the redemption of the dead. What can you think of greater
> than this? To my mind, there isn't anything so great and so
> glorious in this world as to labor for the salvation of the living and

for the redemption of the dead. We read of the Savior going to preach the gospel to the spirits in prison, when his body lay in the tomb. That was a part of the great mission he had to perform. He was sent not only to preach the gospel to those dwelling in mortality, but he was foreordained and anointed of God to open the doors of the prison house to those in bondage and to proclaim his gospel to them.

I have always believed, and still do believe with all my soul, that such men as Peter and James and the twelve disciples chosen by the Savior in his time, have been engaged all the centuries that have passed since their martyrdom for the testimony of Jesus Christ, in proclaiming liberty to the captives in the spirit world and in opening their prison doors. I do not believe that they could be employed in any greater work. Their special calling and anointing of the Lord himself was to save the world, to proclaim liberty to the captives, and the opening of the prison doors to those who were bound in chains of darkness, superstition, and ignorance. I believe that the disciples who have passed away in this dispensation — Joseph, the Prophet, and his brother Hyrum, and Brigham, and Heber, and Willard, and Daniel and John, and Wilford and all the rest of the prophets who have lived in this dispensation, and who have been intimately associated with the work of redemption and the other ordinances of the gospel of the Son of God in this world, are preaching that same gospel that they lived and preached here, to those who are in darkness in the spirit world and who had not the knowledge before they went. The gospel must be preached to them. We are not perfect without them — they cannot be perfect without us. Now, among all these millions of spirits that have lived on the earth and have passed away, from generation to generation, since the beginning of the world, without the knowledge of the gospel — among them you may count that at least one-half are women. Who is going to preach the gospel to the women? Who is going to carry the testimony of Jesus Christ to the hearts of the women who have passed away without a knowledge of the gospel? Well, to my mind, it is a simple thing. These good sisters who have been set apart, ordained to the work, called to it, authorized by the authority of the holy Priesthood to minister for their sex, in the House of God for the living and for the dead, will be fully authorized and empowered to preach the gospel and minister to the women while the elders and prophets are preaching it to the men. The things we experience here are typical of the things of God and the life beyond us. There is a great similarity between God's purposes as manifested here and his purposes as carried out in his presence and kingdom. Those who are authorized to preach the gospel here and are appointed here to do that work will not be idle after they have passed away, but will continue to exercise the rights that they obtained here under the Priesthood of the Son of God to minister for the salvation of those who have died without a knowledge of the truth. Some of you will understand when I tell you that some of these good women who have passed beyond have actually been anointed queens and priestesses unto God and unto their husbands, to continue their work and to be the mothers of spirits in the world to come. The world does not understand this — they cannot receive it — they do not know what it means, and it is sometimes hard for those who ought to be thoroughly imbued with the spirit of the gospel — even for some of us, to comprehend, but it is true. (Joseph F. Smith, *Gospel Doctrine*, 14th ed. [Deseret Book Co., 1966], pages 459-461.)

The insight given us in this funeral sermon gives us the ability to see and understand more clearly the roles of some women in the world after this life. It is in harmony with the scripture known as the "Vision of the Redemption of the Dead," wherein it is made known by President Joseph F. Smith that the Lord spent his time in the world of spirits "instructing and preparing the faithful spirits of the prophets . . . that they might carry the message of redemption unto all the dead. . . . Among the great and mighty ones who were assembled in this vast congregation of the righteous were Father Adam, . . . and our glorious Mother Eve, with many of her faithful daughters who had lived through the ages and worshiped the true and living God." (D&C 138:36-39.)

The law of compensation started before the world was. It will continue into the eternities. God's scheme of things is eternal. We prepare here for the mansions on high hereafter. In our selected activities and preparations here we should have the end in mind. If women are going to have fundamental roles incident to saving their sisters in the world of spirits they should prepare themselves now. Roles here should be preparatory for roles there. This is clear from the words of the two modern prophets quoted above. And these words indicate also, as on this earth, an equality as between males and females in all the essential aspects of eternal progression.

9

Single LDS Women

Everyone faces his own separate needs and frustrations. The needs and frustrations of a single person are often compounded. In the scriptures we are told: "Neither is the man without the woman, neither the woman without the man, in the Lord." (1 Corinthians 11:11.) Within the Church, with the added concept of celestial marriage as a necessary prerequisite for full exaltation (see D&C 132), internal and social pressures are often great for single women. Divorced women often face a heightened sense of failure because of their sensitivity to the Church's opposition to divorce and because of the prejudices sometimes evidenced against them by Church members. Widows also face special needs as they find themselves lonely at home and in the midst of a church which is centered around the family unit — husbands, wives, and children.

It is one thing to say to a single girl, "Don't feel deprived for being single," and quite another to help her meet her needs. Each person, regardless of marital status, needs to find a fulfilling, meaningful life.

Let's examine a fundamental dilemma for women in the Church: When they begin dating, or at a later age, when marriage becomes a serious practical consideration, should they consider marrying out of the Church?

As early as the days of Brigham Young leaders of the Church have counseled against marrying out of the Church. "Be careful, O, Ye mothers in Israel, and do not teach your daughters . . . to marry out of Israel. Woe to you who do it; you will lose your crowns as sure as God lives." (*Journal of Discourses*, 12:97.)

President Young said that "one of the great mistakes made by the children of Abraham, Isaac and Jacob, [was to] marry with other families, although the Lord had forbidden them to do so." (*Journal of Discourses*, 16:111.) They lost the fulness of the gospel because they married among the Gentiles.

In characteristic manner President Young had reason and experience to support his point of view. His reasoning is as sound today as when he instructed the Saints. As a committed Christian he could not understand how one could love a person — love so as to want to marry — if the person so loved was of a nature and disposition not to accept the saving truths of the gospel. "How is it with you, sisters? Do you distinguish between a man of God and a man of the world? It is one of the strangest things that happens in my existence, to think that any man or woman can love a being that will not receive the truth of heaven. The love this Gospel produces is far above the love of women; it is the love of God — the love of eternity — of eternal lives." (*Journal of Discourses*, 8:199-200.)

My love for my wife, and the apparent love of associates for their spouses, leads me to the same wonderment that President Young expressed. Love, admiration, loyalty, and commitment to one another are all bound up in acceptance of the reality of God in our lives. I do not know how one would want to completely share oneself with another without, at the same time, sharing a faith in the ultimate truths.

The more completely one accepts the saving truths of the gospel the more deep-seated are one's views about celestial marriage. In a general conference President Joseph F. Smith spoke of the importance of celestial marriage.

> I say to you . . . I would rather take one of my children to the grave than I would see him turn away from this Gospel. I would rather take my children to the cemetery, and see them buried in innocence, than I would see them corrupted by the ways of the world. I would rather go myself to the grave than to be associated with a wife outside of the bonds of the new and everlasting covenant. Now, I hold it just so sacred; . . . Some people feel that it does not make very much difference whether a girl marries a man in the Church, full of the faith of the Gospel, or an unbe-

liever. Some of our young people have married outside of the Church; but very few of those who have done it failed to come to grief. I would like to see Latter-day Saint men marry Latter-day Saint women; and Methodists marry Methodists, Catholics marry Catholics, and Presbyterians marry Presbyterians, and so on to the limit. Let them keep within the pale of their own faith and church. There is nothing that I can think of, in a religious way, that would grieve me more intensely than to see one of my boys marry an unbelieving girl, or one of my girls marry an unbelieving man. . . . I would to God that every father in Israel saw it just as I do. . . . (Joseph F. Smith, *Gospel Doctrine*, page 279.)

My father taught his family this same concept; as I teach mine. To take a child to the grave in innocence and purity — knowing that the child will come forth to inherit the fulness of the celestial glory — is proximate sorrow, grievous as it is. To jeopardize eternal salvation is ultimate sorrow.

What comfort is there for the single woman who refuses to accept anything but celestial marriage? It is this. God is perfectly just. Eventually all things will be given to the faithful. Their heart's desires will be realized. This life is short. Eternity is long. President Joseph Fielding Smith has promised the faithful single women that no blessing shall be withheld from them.

You good sisters, who are single and alone, do not fear, do not feel that blessings are going to be withheld from you. You are not under any obligation or necessity of accepting some proposal that comes to you which is distasteful for fear you will come under condemnation. If in your hearts you feel that the gospel is true, and would under proper conditions receive these ordinances and sealing blessings in the temple of the Lord; and that is your faith and your hope and your desire, and that does not come to you now; the Lord will make it up, and you shall be blessed — *for no blessing shall be withheld*.

The Lord will judge you according to the desires of your hearts when blessings are withheld in this life, and he is not going to condemn you for that which you cannot help. (Joseph Fielding Smith, *Doctrines of Salvation*, 2:76.)

Is promised salvation enough? It is the hope of the faithful. "There is no gift greater than the gift of salvation." (D&C 6:13.) Those who obtain it in the highest degree are gods. (See D&C 131:1-4; 132.) Being a single woman carries with it a test of faith. God loves all of his children. Nothing will be withheld from the faithful, but this doctrine takes patience in application. It is part of the long-suffering of this probation.

It is conceded that there are success stories from persons who took the other approach and married out of the Church. In the intimate association of marriage, in the everyday argument of good example, their spouses have been brought into the fold. Whenever these experiences are related, I rejoice. However, my observations over the years lead me to believe that these are the exceptions rather than the rule. For the more part the spouses do not come into the Church, and the member is left the long road of living in marriage without the most fundamental of compatibilities.

My observation and experience leads me to the conservative conclusion that the only safe way for a single person to act, in his or her own interest and in those of potential children, is to either convert his or her intended partner before marriage or not marry that person. Human experience demonstrates that in the courtship days one partner has more influence upon the other in such matters than in the ensuing marriage.

Should a woman marry a man of inferior character just to have the benefits of marriage? Emphatically no! If she does she will discover what many a woman has found out the hard way — that, however much she did not like remaining single, being married to the wrong person is infinitely more miserable.

I return to the thought that an unmarried woman in the Church will ultimately be judged by her righteous desires. President Joseph Fielding Smith explained why this is so:

> According to modern custom, it is the place of the man to take the initiative in the matter of a marriage contract. Women are, by force of such custom, kept in reserve and whether it be right or wrong for a woman to take the lead and offer a proposal of marriage, she feels, and she knows that the public would also feel, that she was acting in a forward and unbecoming manner. This is all wrong, but nevertheless it is the fact. The responsibility therefore rests upon the man.
>
> *No woman will be condemned by the Lord for refusing to accept a proposal which she feels she could not properly accept.* In my judgment it is far better for our good girls to refuse an offer of marriage when they think that the companionship of the man would be disagreeable, or if he is one they do not and believe they cannot learn to love.
>
> If in her heart the young woman accepts fully the word of the Lord, and under proper conditions would abide by the law, but refuses an offer when she fully believes that the conditions

would not justify her in entering a marriage contract, which would bind her forever to one she does not love, she shall not lose her reward. The Lord will judge her by the desires of the heart, and the day will come when the blessings withheld shall be given, though it be postponed until the life to come. (Joseph Fielding Smith, *Doctrines of Salvation*, 2:76-77.)

Living in Salt Lake City, where there are so many superior single women properly motivated toward marriage, I have been surprised at the number of eligible men who apparently are not thus motivated. To me it says something about their degree of gospel understanding or allegiance. I recall, as a bishop, calling in one by one all the men in the ward who seemed to me to be slipping past the proper time of marriage and saying: "When I was assigned as bishop to minister to the needs of the members of this ward associated with a great state university, I was struck by the large numbers of males in their late twenties who remained unmarried. I assumed it was because you didn't understand the gospel. Having worked with you I now know that you do understand the gospel, with its concomitant responsibility of marriage. Searching for a reason for your inactivity in this most important part of life I then determined that you simply didn't have the guts to meet the responsibilities in caring for a wife and family. You must suffer from lack of motivation. Further associations with you have proved this is a false assumption also. You are successful in schooling and work. I am forced to another assumption. I still labor under this third assumption. It is that you have an imbalance in your body chemistry." I got a couple of marriages out of that scolding, but some of these men remain single today. If I were a young woman I'd rather wait for the next world for my eternal companion than marry one of them.

It is interesting to note President Smith's condemnation of the present worldly custom wherein women are "kept in reserve" in the courtship process.

Chastity

Nowhere is there more apparent variance between the world and the gospel than in the area of sexual morality. Like their married counterparts, single persons are not only faced with widely accepted, indeed, constantly advertised, carnal norms of sexual permissiveness; they not only live in a world that is neutral on sex morality; they live in a world that actively promotes and encourages sexual immorality. In the name of anti-sex discrimination even government agencies demand housing the sexes together in state housing facilities, in some instances. Add to this environment the natural biological urges to perpetuate the race and we have a first-class temptation for the single person, the temptation to live an unchaste life.

If one truly understood the dignity and purpose of the human body, one would never defile it. In the premortal estate the spirits, sons and daughters of God, shouted for joy when presented with the opportunity to gain mortal bodies. (See Job 38:7.) It was in this way they were to be enabled to become like their celestial parents. Earth life was a place to prove themselves. (See Abraham 3:26.) After a few years here there was to be a separation of body and spirit called death. In the spirit world this separation is looked upon as a bondage to the spirit. The reuniting of the body and the spirit in the resurrection creates an immortal soul. (See D&C 88:15; 93:33.) The resurrection is a restoration to the type of body one assures for oneself during the earth experience. We will have in the eternities just exactly the kind of body we merit by the level of law we have lived on earth: a celestial body, a terrestrial body, a telestial body, or a body that will not be able to endure any kingdom of glory. (See D&C 76:5-111.) This gospel light and knowledge, which should be known to every Latter-day Saint, is armor in defense of defilement of the body.

The body is the place where one's spirit dwells. It is also where the Spirit of God may dwell. "Know ye not that ye are the temple of God, and that the Spirit of God dwelleth in you? If any man defile the temple of God, him shall God destroy; for the temple of God is holy, which temple ye are." (1 Corinthians 3:16-17; see 2 Corinthians 6:16.) The Christian doctrine is "that your body is the temple of the Holy Ghost . . . , and ye are not your own." (1 Corinthians 6:19.) One who observes the law of chastity keeps the temple of God undefiled to that extent.

There is a more compelling argument for chastity. It is that God has commanded us to be sexually clean. The First Presidency published this to the Church in October, 1942:

> For Adam until now, God has commanded that His children be sexually clean. . . . You who have observed the law of chastity have kept the temples of God undefiled. You can stand unabashed before the Lord. He loves you. He will bestow honor and reward upon you. Every overcoming of temptation brings strength and glory to the soul. . . .
>
> But some of us have forgotten what the Lord has said about these sins. Some of us have failed to teach our children the need for sexual purity. Some teachers have tried to lay bare to our

youth the mysteries of life, and so have robbed the creative act of all the sanctity with which from the beginning God has enshrouded it. These have given no restraining righteous principle in its place. So, with too many, modesty has become a derided virtue, and the sex desire has been degraded to the level of hunger and thirst. From Sodom and Gomorrah until now, sex immorality, with its attendant evils of drink and corruption, has brought low the mightiest of nations, has destroyed powerful peoples, has reduced erring man almost to the level of the beasts of the field.

That we may be reminded of the enormity of the sin of unchastity, it is well that we recall some of the things which the Lord and His prophets have said concerning it.

One of the ten basic principles of Christian society, and accepted by all worshippers of the true God, came to man at Sinai when God wrote with His own finger: "Thou shalt not commit adultery."

... Paul declared to the Ephesians: "For this ye know, that no whoremonger, nor unclean person . . . hath any inheritance in the kingdom of Christ and of God." (Ephesians 5:5.) . . . Jacob, teaching the Nephites, declared: "Wo unto them who commit whoredoms, for they shall be thrust down to hell." (2 Nephi 9:36.)

To us of this Church, the Lord has declared that adulterers should not be admitted to membership (D&C 42:76); that adulterers in the Church, if unrepentant, should be cast out (D&C 42:75), but if repentant should be permitted to remain (D&C 42:74; 42:25) and, He said, "By this ye may know if a man repenteth of his sins — behold, he will confess them and forsake them." (D&C 58:43.) . . .

The doctrine of this Church is that sexual sin — the illicit sexual relations of men and women — stands, in its enormity, next to murder.

The Lord has drawn no essential distinction between fornication, adultery, and harlotry or prostitution. Each has fallen under His solemn and awful condemnation.

You youths of Zion, you cannot associate in non-marital, illicit sex relations, which is fornication, and escape the punishments and the judgments which the Lord has declared against this sin. The day of reckoning will come just as certainly as night follows day. They who would palliate this crime and say that such indulgence is but a sinless gratification of a normal desire, like appeasing hunger and thirst, speak filthiness with their lips. Their counsel leads to destruction; their wisdom comes from the Father of Lies. . . .

The Lord will have only a clean people. (James R. Clark, *Messages of the First Presidency*, 6:174-176.)

In another message the First Presidency wrote:

How glorious and near to the angels is youth that is clean; this youth has joy unspeakable here and eternal happiness hereafter. Sexual purity is youth's most precious possession; it is the foundation of all righteousness. Better dead, clean, than alive, unclean. (James R. Clark, *Messages of the First Presidency*, 6:150.)

In the final analysis God's own fiat transcends all argument.

Consider King David, the chosen and anointed, and Joseph, who was sold into Egypt.

I suppose it was a hot and sultry night. David couldn't sleep. He went to his roof to get a breath of air, "and from the roof he saw a woman washing herself; and the woman was very beautiful to look upon. And David sent and inquired after the woman. And one said, Is not this Bath-sheba . . . the wife of Uriah . . . ? And David . . . took her; and she came in unto him, and he lay with her." (2 Samuel 11:2-4.)

Because he had made holy covenants with the Lord and had great light and authority, David's repentance from this act, and from the conspiring to commit murder that grew out of it, took the rest of his mortal life and a lot more time besides. Even that repentance could not secure for him the exaltation he had forfeited. He praised God for the little comfort he finally got: "For thou wilt not leave my soul in hell." (Psalm 16:10.) That is, David would be in hell, but would come forth in a resurrection after sufficient recompense for his sins. The chief apostle, Peter, was careful to note that, while the ancient prophets were raised in the resurrection, after Christ had risen, David had not been resurrected, "and his sepulchre is with us unto this day." (Acts 2:29.)

Like David, Joseph was a capable person. He was made overseer of his master's house. He was given full authority, and the owner "knew not ought he had, save the bread which he did eat." (Genesis 39:6.) Joseph was a handsome man. "His master's wife . . . spake to Joseph day by day, . . . he hearkened not unto her, to lie by her, or to be with her." (Genesis 39:6-7, 10.) The temptation was ongoing. He could have used some of the sophisticated arguments of today: He wouldn't be taking anything from the woman she wasn't offering; she was a consenting adult; it was her body. He used none of these rationalizations. Joseph was saved because he knew the command of

God. "How then can I do this great wickedness, and sin against God?" Joseph did a wise, if unsophisticated, act. He "fled, and got him out." (Genesis 39:9, 12.) As a result of this and a life of righteousness, he has the promise of full exaltation.

Chastity may be destroyed one step at a time. "Can a man take fire in his bosom, and his clothes not be burned? Can one go upon hot coals, and his feet not be burned?" (Proverbs 6:27-32.) Can women and men be immodest with one another and not get burned? Immodesty shows lack of respect for one's body. It leads to grosser offenses. No one knows the exact point at which one can overcome temptation. When one finds out the outer limits of one's strength, it is too late. It is the height of folly for a person to put himself in a position from which he might not extricate himself.

I conclude this section with the wisdom of President J. Reuben Clark:

> May I say to the youth of the Church, and first to your daughters: That man or youth who demands without marriage as the price of his favor or love the enjoyment of your body, has in fact nothing but sorrow and degradation to give you in return; and next, to you sons: That woman who offers to you her body outside wedlock, invites you to a feast that brings disease and corruption that will pollute you until death. And any man or woman who demands as the price of his favor or friendship a surrender of any of your righteous standards of living, is offering to you nothing worth buying. What it brings is false as Evil itself. (*Conference Report*, April 1940, page 22.)

Enlarging Your Sphere of Usefulness

Some women, because they feel deprived by being single, do very little with life. (For that matter, so do some married women, for other reasons.) Single women's lives are just as important as non-single women's lives. As with every man, every woman is under an obligation to make for herself a meaningful life.

One way to get away from the self-pity of feeling deprived is to understand that sex roles have been vastly overdone. Brigham Young tried to expand men's and women's minds in this matter. "The ladies can learn to keep books as well as the men; we have some few, already, who are just as good accountants as many of our brethren. Why not teach more to keep books and sell goods, and let them do this business." (*Journal of Discourses*, 12:374-75.) On another occasion he said: "We believe that women are useful, not only to sweep houses, wash dishes, make beds, and raise babies, but they should stand behind the counter, study law or physic... to enlarge their sphere of usefulness for the benefit of society at large. In following these things they but answer the design of their creation." (*Journal of Discourses,* 13:61.)

To "enlarge their sphere of usefulness"; now, that is the key! All of us, male or female, married or single, should be about the business of enlarging ourselves and our usefulness. "Verily, I say, men should be anxiously engaged in a good cause, and do many things of their own free will, and bring to pass much righteousness; for the power is in them, wherein they are agents unto themselves. And inasmuch as men do good they shall in nowise lose their reward." (D&C 58:27-28.)

There is much to be done. Those who put love of God in the center of their lives attain a sense of spirituality. They develop a serenity and a wholeness in their lives. The highest manifestation of love is found in a person's devotion to God. (See Deuteronomy 6:5, Matthew 22:37-38.) The second highest manifestation of love is found in a person's attitude toward his fellow beings. (See Matthew 22:39.)

Love is always the partner of service. It is through service that love is manifest. If love be the precept, then service is the example. As King Benjamin put it: "When ye are in the service of your fellow beings ye are only in the service of your God." (Mosiah 2:17.)

How many service projects are yet undone? How much charitable work? Use the gospel in your lives. Set virtuous goals. Develop self-discipline. Make a contribution to humankind. Forget yourselves in the service of your God. You will find a newness of life. Said the Savior, "He that loseth his life for my sake shall find it." (Matthew 10:39.)

And that "finding," in the case of the righteous single girl, will culminate in a future sphere where all wrongs will be righted, all unfairness abolished, and all righteous womanly desires brought to glorious fulfillment.

10

Modern Women in the Church

One of the tides of our times is the feeling among many women that they have been assigned; and they have accepted, the lesser tasks and roles in our society. It would not be realistic to say that the overwash of this tide has not reached the Saints. Let us consider some of the responsibilities of women in the Church today.

The Special Role of Wife

A wife might say to her husband, "You are the bishop (or the stake president, or whatever) because I allow and encourage you to be." She would be correct. A husband cannot properly perform time-consuming and energy-draining Church or civic services unless his wife frees him from some domestic responsibilities by assuming them herself. That is part of the proper marriage relationship. The husband nurtures the wife and, in large measure because of her willing use of special talents, she enables him to be "known in the gates, when he sitteth among the elders of the land." (Proverbs 31:23.)

Wives are meant to be honored by their husbands; that is, they are to be held in high esteem and accorded respectful regard. In part, this results as wives manifest talents to help their husbands.

A wife's responsibility to her husband is primary to her responsibility to her children. This is a gospel principle. The earliest of scriptures on this carries God's directive in the first person: "Unto the woman he said, . . . thy desire shall be to thy husband." (Genesis 3:16.) This means that to be a successful wife a woman must be primarily more concerned about her husband's wants than she is about her children's wants. She is a wife first and a mother second.

Love and the sexual expression of that love in marriage is a vital part of a happy marriage. Connubial love should be enjoyed as an expression of love. It may even be sanctifying. "Sexual union is lawful in wedlock, and if participated in with right intent is honorable and sanctifying." (Joseph F. Smith, *Gospel Doctrine,* page 309.)

Husbands and wives, having kept themselves chaste and modest through courtship, sometimes are slow in establishing satisfying marital relationships. The Church does not supply detailed instructions on this delicate and loving companionship. Part of the reward for premarital modesty is discovery together. Marriage, however, does not make proper certain extremes in sexual indulgence. Life is not designed just for sex, and marriage partners have responsibilities one to the other in this regard.

Sexual intimacies are to be between the husband and wife only. One of the ends of conjugal love is to "be fruitful, and multiply, and replenish the earth." (Genesis 1:28.) However, this is not the only proper end to such union. Expressions and acts of love should be mutually pleasurable, for this satisfies one of their purposes.

Successful women are industrious, applying the great principle of work. The Old Testament definition of a "virtuous woman" is still true and applicable.

> She seeketh wool, and flax, and worketh willingly with her hands.
>
> She is like the merchants' ships; she bringeth her food from afar.
>
> She riseth also while it is yet night, and giveth meat to her household, and a portion to her maidens.
>
> She considereth a field, and buyeth it: with the fruit of her hands she planteth a vineyard.
>
> She girdeth her loins with strength, and strengtheneth her arms.
>
> She perceiveth that her merchandise is good: her candle goeth not out by night.
>
> She layeth her hands to the spindle, and her hands hold the distaff.

She stretcheth out her hand to the poor; yea, she reacheth forth her hands to the needy.

She is not afraid of the snow for her household: for all her household are clothed with scarlet.

She maketh herself coverings of tapestry; her clothing is silk and purple. . . .

She maketh fine linen, and selleth it; and delivereth girdles unto merchants. (Proverbs 31:13-22, 24.)

Men, women, spirits, angels, and gods are to use their physical and mental powers to work. Jesus said: "My Father worketh hitherto, and I work." (John 5:17.) "I must work the works of him that sent me, while it is day." (John 9:4.) Without work there would be nothing. There would be neither creation nor temporal necessities nor salvation. God worked six days in the creation of this earth and then rested the seventh day. (See Exodus 20:8-11.) The Father's work and glory is "to bring to pass the immortality and eternal life of man." (Moses 1:39.) Our Lord's mission was to work out the infinite and eternal atonement. (See 3 Nephi 27:13-15.) Men and women are commanded to work both temporally and spiritually. (See Genesis 3:19; Philippians 2:12.) Work is a great blessing and idleness is a curse — for either males or females.

Motherhood

In Latter-day Saint theology and religion motherhood is an exalted position. One who gives birth to a child is the origin or source of something wonderful. As she properly nurtures her children and assumes the full responsibilities and character of a mother, she continues to find fulfillment as a woman. *Mother* is a title of affectionate respect. Motherhood is viewed as the primary role of womankind in the Church.

Patriarchal blessings of many faithful women give the inspired promise that they will be mothers in Israel. This expression has two meanings: It means motherhood in the house of Israel here in mortality, and it means motherhood among exalted beings in eternity. These two concepts are tied together. Motherhood in this life brings forth natural offspring. Faith and devotion on the part of the mothers in latter-day Israel in rearing their children in light and truth means the opportunity to have the family unit continue into eternity, including the creation of eternal lives by bringing forth spirit children. (See D&C 131:1-4; 132:19-32.) I know of no greater incentive to mothers than this promise: They may be mothers in heaven.

Implicit in the Christian verity that all men are the spirit children of an *Eternal Father* is the usually unspoken truth that they are also the offspring of an *Eternal Mother.* An exalted and glorified Man of Holiness (Moses 6:57) could not be a Father unless a Woman of like glory, perfection, and holiness was associated with him as a Mother. The begetting of children makes a man a father and a woman a mother whether we are dealing with man in his mortal or immortal state. (Bruce R. McConkie, *Mormon Doctrine,* page 516.)

This glorious doctrine of celestial parentage, of a Father *and* mother in heaven, emphasizes the true equality of opportunity between the sexes in LDS theology. It also serves to illustrate the exalted position of motherhood in the scheme of things.

While the priesthood is given only to the men in the Church, its benefits and blessings are shared by their wives and family. Elder John A. Widtsoe aptly put it:

In the ordinances of the Priesthood man and woman share alike. The temple doors are open to every faithful member of the Church. And, it is to be noted that the highest blessings therein available are only conferred upon a man and woman, husband and wife, jointly. Neither can receive them alone. In the Church of Christ, woman is not an adjunct to, but an equal partner with man. (John A. Widstoe, "The 'Mormon' Woman," *Relief Society Magazine,* June-July 1943, page 373.)

Elder Bruce R. McConkie, in discussing the doctrine recorded in Doctrine and Covenants 131:1-4, makes this significant statement:

[Man] cannot attain a fulness of joy here or of eternal reward hereafter alone. Woman stands at his side a joint-inheritor with him in the fulness of all things. Exaltation and eternal increase is her lot as well as his. (Bruce R. McConkie, *Mormon Doctrine,* page 844.)

Among the great doctrines of the Church, none is perhaps more sublime or more comforting to women than the doctrine of the eternity of the family. According to the late President J. Reuben Clark, Jr., the Latter-day Saint family has three fundamental functions:

First, — it must bring to its members such lives as will enable them to return to the inner circles of that celestial home from which they came, — a dwelling with the Heavenly Father and Mother throughout the eternities.

Second, — it must so carry out its duties, rights, and functions as to enable it, in turn, to found a celestial home that shall in some eternity hereafter be equal in power, opportunity, and dignity with the celestial home from which we came and to which we shall return.

Third, — it must so live its life as to provide for the spirits yet waiting to come to this earth for their fleshly tabernacles, both bodies and minds that shall be healthy, for the spirits coming through them are the choice spirits, which have earned the right by their lives in their first estate, to come for their second estate, to the righteous homes — to the families of greatest worth, promise, and opportunity; and this family must provide for this spirit which it invites to come to its hearthstone, an environment that shall meet the strictest requirements of righteousness. (J. Reuben Clark, "Our Homes," *Relief Society Magazine*, December 1940, page 808.)

Among the Saints, the role of motherhood is equated as a partnership with God. It is an indispensable ingredient of giving earthly tabernacles to his spirit children and then preparing these children to return to him. No other profession or honor is the equivalent of motherhood.

Parents are equally responsible to train their children.

And again, inasmuch as parents have children in Zion, or in any of her stakes which are organized, that teach them not to understand the doctrine of repentance, faith in Christ the Son of the living God, and of baptism and the gift of the Holy Ghost by the laying on of the hands, when eight years old, the sin be upon the heads of the parents.

For this shall be a law unto the inhabitants of Zion, or in any of her stakes which are organized. . . .

And they shall also teach their children to pray, and to walk uprightly before the Lord. (D&C 68:25-28.)

Much of a family's rearing rests with the mother because of the father's responsibility to provide the necessities of life for the family. As a stake president, I invited the late President Joseph Fielding Smith to a banquet for the leadership of the stake the evening before quarterly conference commenced. He commented on the challenge women face in rearing children in righteousness. He said that as a practical matter "the sisters do about 90 percent of the training and rearing of the children." From the head table, in a stage whisper for all to hear, my wife said to me, "I wonder who does the other 10 percent."

The lives and contributions of the children are the measure of the mother. This is her greatest Church, civic, cultural, or other service. A story from Roman history comes to mind. Cornelia, a Roman matron, had twelve children, three of whom survived — a daughter, and two sons whom history refers to as the Gracchi. (Gracchus was the family name.) These sons so distinguished themselves as soldiers, reformers, and statesmen that a great statue was erected in recognition of their service. But the statue was not erected to the sons themselves. Rather, it was erected to the mother who bore and reared them. On it were inscribed these words: "To Cornelia, mother of the Gracchi."

The greatness of the role given to mothers must be seen in its eternal setting to be appreciated. Eternal life begins at home.

Parents have the primary responsibility to help save their own families. Because the mother is with the children more hours of each day than is the father, she becomes their major trainer. This can be both an opportunity and a burden. Joseph F. Smith, sixth president of the Church, taught in a funeral sermon of Sister Mary A. Freeze:

> Now, may the Lord bless Brother Freeze. As Sister Martha Tingey has said, Sister Freeze could never have done the work she has done if it had not been for his seconding her in her efforts. He consented to her partially neglecting her home duties in order to labor in a broader field for the salvation of others. But just here let me say a word to you mothers. Oh, mothers, salvation, mercy, life everlasting begin at home. "What profiteth it a man, though he gain the whole world and lose his own soul?" What would it profit me, though I should go out into the world and win strangers to the fold of God and lose my own children? Oh! God, let me not lose my own. I can not afford to lose mine, whom God has given to me and whom I am responsible for before the Lord, and who are dependent upon me for guidance, for instruction, for proper influence. Father, do not permit me to lost interest in my own, in trying to save others. Charity begins at home. Life everlasting should begin at home. I should feel very badly to be made to realize, by and by, that through my neglect of home, while trying to save others, I have lost my own. I do not want that. The Lord help me to save my own, so far as one can help another. I realize I cannot save anybody, but I can teach them how to be saved. I can set an example before my children how they can be saved, and it is my duty to do that first. I owe it more to them than to anybody else in the world. Then, when I have accomplished the work I should do in my own home circle, let me extend my power for good abroad just as far as I can. (Joseph F. Smith, *Gospel Doctrine*, pages 461-62.)

Mothers cannot do everything. Other meritorious service and personal contributions are secondary to saving one's family. Indeed, a mother performs her best service for such social institutions as reform schools by keeping her children out of them. Her best act for society as a whole is her contribution of individual citizens in each of her children.

Elder Thomas S. Monson restated the role of mothers in Church terms as expressive as any I know: " 'One cannot forget mother and remember God. One cannot remember mother and forget God.' Why? Because these two sacred persons, God and mother, partners in creation, in love, in sacrifice, in service, are as one." (Thomas S. Monson, *Behold Thy Mother* [Deseret Book Co., 1967].)

Women's Place in the Church

The Latter-day Saint woman has a significant role in the affairs of the Church. From the beginning days of the Church women have been given voice in the affairs of the Church. They have voted side by side with men on all questions submitted to the general Church membership for vote. This recognition was an advanced concept in 1830 when no women had political franchise. The will of the Lord in this matter was made clear in a revelation given to the Prophet Joseph Smith at Harmony, Pennsylvania, in July, 1830, three months after the Church was organized. The Lord said: "And all things shall be done by common consent in the church." (D&C 26:2.) "The church" had been defined by the Lord as "whosoever repenteth and cometh unto me, the same is my church." (D&C 10:67.) Male and female are thus treated alike in this matter.

It is anticipated that woman will lend her full strength, according to her nature and in harmony with God's system, to the building of the kingdom of God on earth. She commits herself in the selfsame sacred covenant as does the male. At baptism each covenants "to come into the fold of God, and to be called his people, . . . to bear one another's burdens, . . . to mourn with those that mourn; [to] comfort those that stand in need of comfort, and to stand as witnesses of God at all times and in all things, and in all places." (Mosiah 18:8-9.) Part of her purpose in being here is to consecrate her time, talents, and means to building the kingdom of God. In addition to fulfilling this by her roles as wife and mother, she serves in Church callings.

In the beginning God revealed his purposes in creating men and women. "For behold, this is my work and my glory — to bring to pass the immortality and eternal life of man." (Moses 1:39.) God's stated purpose is the purpose of his Church. The work of the Church is divided into three general categories: perfecting the Saints, genealogical research and temple work, and missionary work. The work thus fits the purpose. We are to see that we get saved, that our kindred, living and dead, have opportunity of salvation, and that everyone else hears the gospel and has the opportunity to be saved. Mormon women actively participate in all this work of the Church.

Women have all sorts of roles in perfecting the Saints. They serve in all of the auxiliaries of the Church, completely staffing the Relief Society, completely or substantially staffing the Primary, teaching most of the Sunday School classes, and teaching and superintending young women's activities in the youth programs of the Church.

Relief Society membership is numbered in the hundreds of thousands. As Relief Society members, women render untold hours of compassionate service. They are an indispensable part of the Church welfare system, where on a grass roots level welfare aid is dispensed by Relief Society presidents and by bishops. Certainly women are heavily involved in the business of perfecting the Saints.

Belle S. Spafford, former leader of combined international women's organizations and former president of the Relief Society, wrote:

> It was the desire to increase woman's usefulness to the Church that led the sisters of Nauvoo to approach the Prophet and seek to be organized. They had been zealous in their service as individuals, but they felt greatly limited in working as such. It must have been comforting to them when Eliza R. Snow, having represented them before the Prophet in their request for an organization, conveyed to them these meaningful words of the Prophet: "Tell the sisters their offering is accepted of the Lord. . . . I will organize them under the priesthood after a pattern of the priesthood."
>
> With the growth and expansion of the Church, the contribution of the women has been multiplied a thousandfold over that of the sisters of Nauvoo. As we contemplate the blessings enjoyed by Latter-day Saint women today — greater perhaps than those enjoyed by any other single body of women — may we not feel the contribution of the women of this day is accepted of the Lord? (Belle S. Spafford, *Women in Today's World* [Deseret Book Co., 1971], pages 237-38.)

Women work beside men in all parts of genealogical research. There is no way to determine who contributes most to genealogical research. Men and women are equally responsible for this work. Together or separately they research matriarchal and patriarchal lines alike.

Women and men work side by side in performing the various ordinances of work for the dead in the temples of the Church. Approximately the same numbers of males and females have their work done for them in the temples, and both men and women are ordained and do perform these sacred ordinances of exaltation for the dead.

Women have two roles in the missionary work of the Church. Mothers inspire their sons and daughters to want to do missionary service and train them so that they can do the work effectively. Women also serve as proselyting missionaries. Women and men are set apart to serve full-time tours of duty as missionaries. Everyone in the Church has a like responsibility to teach the gospel and to fellowship new converts. All should provide financial assistance to the missionary cause.

President Heber J. Grant, seventh President of the Church, generously praised the women, but spoke accurately when he said: "Without the wonderful work of the women I realize that the Church would have been a failure." (G. Homer Durham, comp., *Gospel Standards* [Salt Lake City: *Improvement Era*, 1943], page 150.)

The place of women in the Church, having been defined by divine decree, does not materially change. It remains constant. It is the same today as it was yesterday. It will be substantially the same tomorrow. Inasmuch as women function in the Church as God intends, this is a great source of fulfillment. The rewards come both here and now as well as in the eternities to come.

Women's Frustrations in the Church

Mortality is a time of testing, a time of struggle, and, it is hoped, a time of growth. It is a time for us to overcome, and in some matters women have to overcome more than men.

In my judgment the biggest single frustration that women have in the Church is the attitude that many men hold, the attitude of superiority.

The Prophet Joseph Smith enunciated this true observation of human nature: "We have learned by sad experience that it is the nature and disposition of almost all men, as soon as they get a little authority, as they suppose, they will immediately begin to exercise unrighteous dominion." (D&C 121:39.)

The Lord has always designated those who shall hold his power and authority. The power and authority of God as delegated to mankind is called *priesthood.* It is a heavenly calling. God designated Adam (see Moses 6:67-68) and a succession of men, as recorded in the scriptures and to this very day, to hold his priesthood. It is he who establishes eligibility. It is apparent that in the divine division of labor it was man's responsibility and burden to bear the priesthood.

Some of us men like to reflect, with considerable self-satisfaction, that the priesthood to which we are ordained was called by the senior of the apostles in the time of Jesus "a royal priesthood" and makes of us "the people of God." (See 1 Peter 2:9-10.) It is often easier to contemplate this than to act out our designated role as servants doing the works of the Master with his delegated power and authority. (See John 14:12-13.) We would do better to contemplate less on the fact that we were "called of God" (see Hebrews 5:4) and to concern ourselves more with the reason we were called. We were called to serve. Priesthood is a service calling. Its bearers are to serve all of God's children, male and female alike. The responsibility is one of service.

All of God's children are to receive the blessings administered through the priesthood. These blessings may be present or future. Women receive all of the present blessings: blessing and naming as infants, father's blessings, baptism, confirmation and bestowal of the gift of the Holy Ghost, blessings for health and comfort and strength, patriarchal blessings, endowments, celestial marriage, sealings, having one's calling and election made sure, and dedication of graves. Women receive the future blessings contingent upon being found worthy in final judgment: a better resurrection, and exaltation. Men and women will and do enjoy, equally, present and future priesthood blessings.

Why, then, do many men still have attitudes of superiority? I think it is because we haven't educated and trained the brethren sufficiently. They are called and set apart from the rest of the world at the early age of twelve years. In attempting to help them honor the priesthood, we have tended to honor them as males. The attitude that they are special has been planted. It takes considerable spiritual maturity and an integrated personality to take this heady treatment without getting puffed up. I think it is fair to say that many of the brethren, who are otherwise disciplined Christians, exercise unrighteous dominion over women.

We bring the sisters in when their brothers are ordained to the priesthood. Their thinking is shaped also by this event. But care should be taken to use this teaching moment to build up the girls as well as the boys. All should know they count equally.

Part of the male's attitude in this respect is unconscious. He doesn't think he is acting "superior." At a high-level Church work committee meeting one of the women made the major contributions in developing programs and solving problems. One of the men thought he was complimenting her as he said at the conclusion of meeting: "I like what you say. You think just like a man!"

But part of men's attitudes in this area comes from conscious behavior. Some men think they are superior to women because they have been given the priesthood and women have not. It doesn't assuage the frustration of women for me to say to such men that they should read the revelation on how to use priesthood. "No power or influence can or ought to be maintained by virtue of the priesthood, only by persuasion, by long-suffering, by gentleness and meekness, and by love unfeigned; by kindness, and pure knowledge, which shall greatly enlarge the soul without hypocrisy, and without guile." (D&C 121:41-42.) It is precisely because of an attitude contrary to this counsel that many men "are called, but few are chosen." (D&C 121:40.)

If women understand the proper concept, this understanding should help them in dealing with some men's obnoxious attitudes. But a woman should be able to separate the issue from the unperceptive man's response to it. She ought not to be overly sensitive to the issue itself. Certainly any priesthood bearer with even modest mental and spiritual understanding will recognize the divine division of labor in which women are given the responsibility of childbearing and the requisite special aptitudes and talents to love and rear children, and he will acknowledge that this is as important and selective a designation of duty as is that of bearing the priesthood. In my experience, a woman who is nurtured and taught in love, who is secure and prepared by understanding, either is not bothered by or overcomes any frustrations on the score of priesthood bearing.

But women also face other possible frustrations stemming from the competition for time and strength between the home and the Church.

When I was ordained to the office of a bishop and set apart to preside over a ward, my wife was carrying our first child. Apostolic hands were laid upon my head and the duties and responsibilities and challenges of the bishopric were recited to me. Toward the end of the ordination blessing, I was given this counsel: "Remember, your first obligation is to your wife and family."

I was then a young lawyer trying to establish a professional standing. My wife was about to have the first of our eight children. My energies were now divided again in priesthood service. My wife was left with the added burdens of bearing and rearing our children with less of my time available to do my part at home. This competition for time and strength is repeated ten thousand times each day in the Church.

Every "Church wife" asks herself sometimes — as her husband hurriedly leaves a dinner table surmounted with unwashed dishes and surrounded by tired children ready to be put to bed — Is this Church meeting really necessary? The Scoutmaster who takes part of his annual vacation to take the Scout troop camping has a wife and family, too. So does the elders quorum president. There is no ready answer to these problems.

Add to this competition the demands Church callings make on the woman's time and energies. Most Relief Society and Primary officers and teachers have families. Frequently, knowing that the family is supposed to come first merely adds to one's frustrations in fulfilling Church calls and obligations.

It is true that one finds satisfaction and fulfillment in Church service, but it is also true that Church service is sometimes used as an excuse to neglect the weightier matters of family rearing and responsibilities. Successful husbands and wives carefully work out proper balances in these matters.

Church service should help parents in the rearing of their children. First, it expands the parents as individuals as they become more loving and giving persons. Second, it helps children make love of God and mankind the center of their lives if they see their mother's and father's example before them. But the parents must do these things in wisdom.

What was said in my ordination blessing was true. It was inept application of this principle that was sometimes faulty. Working out a balanced program is a very individual thing. Various levels of health and strength, of emotional stability, and other individual needs must be taken into consideration. It is not easy. This is an area where the Church can complicate one's life and make it more difficult. The solution is to start where you are and work on the best solution to your individual problems.

The Spectrum of Choice

We have previously discussed the difficulty in defining roles between males and females. Circumstances vary. There is a variance of personality and physical strength. We have discussed exemplary women as mothers, wives, queens, missionaries, genealogists, prophetesses, pioneers, social and political activists, business women, authors, and as charitable and Church workers. We could add to this painters, musicians, dancers, educators, and an almost endless list. Women have a broad selection of choice. The very breadth of the spectrum often brings frustrations.

There is the mother who never had the opportunity to finish her university degree. She had six children, served as a ward president of both the Primary Association and the Relief Society, served as a senior member of the General Board of the Relief Society, gave such civic service as that of president of the local PTA and state chairman of a war bond campaign, and sustained her husband under demanding circumstances. Yet she felt she had missed something. When the last of her children was mature enough to allow it, she spent her summers working on the credit hours to finish her degree.

There is the girl who graduated from a university with a cumulative grade point average of 3.999 on a 4.0 scale. She married while she and her husband were still in school and saw her husband through postgraduate professional school. She has two sons, is pregnant, and has a driving desire to get her master's degree.

How does a woman satisfy her needs and desires? The desire for one activity frequently seems to thwart another desire. Given pre-earth training, divine directives, unique physiological potential, sensitive natures, conscious and unconscious needs, and otherwise equal abilities with men, she has the component parts for possible frustration. Her attempts to define her role and her potential are part of her greatest challenges. It is worth observing, however, that some of this is merely a matter of making choices. For either men or women, this is largely what life is all about — choosing as between good and bad or, as perhaps more appropriate to this discussion, between courses representing differing degrees of good and of long-term satisfaction.

Women in the Church have been given some guidelines to help them order their lives. One of the great thrusts of the gospel is its emphasis upon woman's natural roles, and attempts to change these roles are seen as "Satan and his cohorts . . . using . . . nefarious propaganda to lure women away from their primary responsibilities as wives, mothers, and homemakers." (N. Eldon Tanner, *Ensign*, January 1974, page 7.) Wives and mothers are encouraged to make their husbands and children their first concern.

President Spencer W. Kimball restates this guideline:

> Of late years, mothers have left their homes to work in such numbers that Church authorities are much concerned, and make a call to mothers: "Come back home, Mothers, come back home." We realize that there is an occasional mother who must

go out to work. There are some mothers whose children are all reared, and who are thus free to work. But for mothers to leave children when there is not an absolute necessity is a hazardous thing. Generally, children just cannot grow up properly disciplined under babysitters, no matter how good they may be, as they can under a mother who loves them so much that she would die for them. (Spencer W. Kimball, *The Miracle of Forgiveness*, page 254.)

From my observation (my wife being a mother of eight children and a superb homemaker), those persons who say that mothering and homemaking isn't challenging enough for them simply do not understand the role of mother and homemaker. It is demanding. It is constant. It is all-consuming. It takes imagination; my wife generates more alternative solutions in a day than I do as a lawyer in my office. Fulfilling the roles of wife, mother, and homemaker has its rewards. Accepting and fulfilling these roles helps assuage frustrations.

One does not need to make decisions over and over again. When a woman bears a child, she has made many decisions. Once she has accepted the responsibility to rear the child, she shouldn't remake the decision each day. She should fulfill her decision to rear the child. Until that child is properly reared, she should not abandon her decision and commitment, but should seek contentment in her role.

Through the spectrum of roles the overriding caution remains: "But always remember that home and children come first and must not be neglected." (N. Eldon Tanner, *Ensign*, January 1974, page 10.)

An Elect Lady

Among the righteous the goal is exaltation, so the desire is to have one's calling and election made sure. What is meant by calling? And who are called of God? To be called is to be a faithful member of the Church and kingdom of God on earth. It is to be numbered with the Saints. It is to be a son or daughter of the Lord Jesus Christ. " . . . All those who receive my gospel are sons and daughters in my kingdom." (D&C 25:1.)

The call originates with God. It is available to all men and women. (See Mark 16:15-16.) Paul repeatedly uses the terminology "called to be saints." (See Romans 1:7; 1 Corinthians 1:2.) The Saints are called . . . out of darkness into [the] marvellous light" of the gospel. (1 Peter 2:9.) They are "called" to suffer in the course of righteousness, that thereby they "should inherit a blessing." (1 Peter 2:21; 3:9.)

What is meant by election? Who are the elect of God? To what have they been elected? Election is synonymous with calling. The Lord and his apostles speak of the elect as the true Saints, as the faithful believers, as those who love the Lord and are seeking to do his will. (See Matthew 24:22; Mark 13:20; Colossians 3:12; 2 Timothy 2:10.) In our day, the Lord has promised to gather and save his elect. (See D&C 29:7; 33:6; 35:20.)

> *What is meant by making an election sure?*
> It is with election as with calling: the chosen of the Lord are offered all of the blessings of the gospel on the condition of obedience to the Lord's laws; and they, having been tried and tested and found worthy in all things, eventually have a seal placed on their election which guarantees the receipt of the promised blessing.
> *What is meant by having one's calling and election made sure?*
> To have one's calling and election made sure is to be sealed up unto eternal life; it is to have the unconditional guarantee of exaltation in the highest heaven of the celestial world; it is to receive the assurance of Godhood; it is, in effect, to have the day of judgment advanced, so that an inheritance of all the glory and honor of the Father's kingdom is assured prior to the day when the faithful actually enter into the divine presence to sit with Christ in his throne. (Bruce R. McConkie, *Doctrinal New Testament Commentary,* 3:330-31.)

Peter counseled: "Make your calling and election sure: for if ye do these things, ye shall never fall." (2 Peter 1:10.) Joseph Smith's teachings are the same: "Go on and continue to call upon God until you make your calling and election sure." (Joseph Smith, *Teachings of the Prophet Joseph Smith,* page 299.)

Emma Smith, the Prophet's wife, had a revelation from God defining her duties and explaining some of the blessings that would follow her faithfulness. The Lord called her "an elect lady." (D&C 25:3.) Although the revelation spoke directly to her, it also clearly helps women in general in defining their roles. God said: "And the office of thy calling shall be for a comfort unto my servant, Joseph Smith, Jun., thy husband, in his afflictions, with consoling words, in the spirit of meekness." (D&C 25:5.)

A discussion of modern women in the Church would not be complete without giving this statement a central position. The "office and calling" of Joseph's wife was a supporting role to his work.

However, Emma was given other obligations. She was "to expound the scriptures, and to exhort the Church." (D&C 25:7.) She was told that her "time [was to] be given to writing, and to learning much." (D&C 25:8.) In addition to these general admonitions, she was required to do two specific tasks, one for her husband and one for the Church. She was to "go with" her husband and be his "scribe" (D&C 25:6), and she was "to make a selection of sacred hymns . . . to be had in [the Lord's] church." (D&C 25:11.)

All women have both general and specific responsibilities, but of particular interest is the injunction to Emma to "expound scriptures" and "exhort the church" to righteous living. Having opened the doors of private and public service, the revelation then cautions: "Continue in the spirit of meekness, and beware of pride. Let thy soul delight in thy husband, and the glory which shall come upon him" (D&C 25:14.) With all the wife's responsibilities and obligations she should find her primary fulfillment with her husband in the Church. If she does this continually, in conjunction with keeping the Lord's other commandments, she will receive "a crown of righteousness." However, if she fails to do this, the Lord says, "Where I am you cannot come." (D&C 25:15.)

For a woman, these instructions become part of making her calling and election sure.

11

Exaltation and Godhood

It is the first principle of the gospel to know for a certainty the character of God." (Joseph Smith, *History of the Church*, 6:305.) The Prophet Joseph continued, "When we understand the character of God, and know how to come to Him, he begins to unfold the heavens to us, and to tell us all about it. When we are ready to come to him, he is ready to come to us." (Joseph Smith, *History of the Church*, 6:308.)

Peter tells us how to know God and to draw nigh unto him. He tells us: "It is written, Be ye holy; for I am holy." (1 Peter 1:16.) He says we should be "partakers of the divine nature." (2 Peter 1:4.) That is, we should observe the attributes of God and then commence to make the attributes of his character our own.

In the revelations God has given the human family, we find the following account of the attributes of God. Joseph Smith lists them in the Third and Fourth Lectures in his *Lectures on Faith*.

1. Knowledge. "Known unto God are all his works from the beginning of the world." (Acts 15:15.) God knows all things. He even has a "foreknowledge of all things." (Alma 13:7.)
2. Faith or Power. "The Lord of hosts hath sworn, saying, Surely, as I have thought, so shall it come to pass; and as I have purposed, so shall it stand." (Isaiah 14:24, 27.) "Through

faith we understand that the worlds were framed by the word of God." (Hebrews 11:3.) God possesses power and faith.

3. Justice. "Justice and judgment are the habitation of thy throne." (Psalm 89:14.) "Behold, thy King cometh unto thee: he is just, and having salvation." (Zechariah 9:9.) God is a dispenser of justice.

4. Judgment. "He is the Rock, his work is perfect: for all his ways are judgment: a God of truth and without iniquity, just and right is he." (Deuteronomy 32:4.) God dispenses judgment. He is just.

5. Mercy. "Mercy and truth shall go before [his] face." (Psalm 89:14.) "But thou art a God ready to pardon, gracious and merciful." (Nehemiah 9:17.)

6. Truth. "A God of truth. . . ." (Deuteronomy 32:4.) "Into thine hand I commit my spirit: thou hast redeemed me, O Lord God of truth." (Psalm 31:5.) All truth is centered in God, who is the source of all truth. (*Lectures on Faith,* comp. N. B. Lundwall, Lecture Three [Bookcraft, Inc.], pages 41-42.)

God is perfect in all of his attributes. "What we mean by the perfections [of God] is, the perfections which belong to all the attributes of his nature." (N. B. Lundwall, *Lectures on Faith,* Lecture Five, page 48.) One of his attributes is knowledge. He is perfect in all of his attributes. Therefore, he possesses perfect knowledge. He knows everything. His understanding is perfect.

If we are to be partakers of the divine nature as pertaining to knowledge, we must gain knowledge. Little as we feel we may learn, we must start.

One of the attributes of God is faith. Being perfect in all attributes, he has perfect faith. If we are to put on the divine nature, we must develop faith.

Justice, judgment, and mercy are his attributes. So we must be just and merciful to put on the divine nature.

God is the very embodiment of love. "He that loveth not knoweth not God; for God is love." (1 John 4:8.) We must commence to love. This is the way to know God. This is the way to be like him. He is perfect in love, and although we are not perfect in our present state, we must begin.

One of the attributes of God is truth. "God is not a man, that he should lie." (Numbers 23:19.) He is a God of truth and cannot lie. If we are to be partakers of his nature, we must be truthful. We must not lie.

In all of these characteristics of God, in all of these attributes of God, men and women are alike in their potential. God is no respecter of persons. Peter said, "Of a truth I perceive that God is no respecter of persons: . . . he that feareth him, and worketh righteousness, is accepted with him." (Acts 10:34-35.) These are the essential characteristics of humankind. In these, men and women are one. These are the common denominators. Compared to those unities, physiological differences are insignificant.

There is no double standard in the gospel. There is not one plan of salvation for men and another for women. All of the human family are given the same laws and ordinances. We are all judged by the same criteria. Jesus did not conclude his Sermon on the Mount by saying to the women only, or to the men only, "Be ye therefore perfect, even as your Father which is in heaven is perfect." (Matthew 5:48.) If anyone is to be the manner of person Jesus is, he must alike abide the Savior's precepts.

One of the names of God is Eternal. "Eternal is my name." (Moses 7:35.) When the scriptures talk about eternal life, they usually mean the type and quality of life *Eternal* (God) possesses. This is much more than living forever. It has to do with ultimate fulfillment. It is to be a joint heir with Jesus Christ. This full heirship cannot be had separately for either men or women: "Neither is the man without the woman, neither the woman without the man, in the Lord." (1 Corinthians 11:11.) Men and women are dependent on one another for exaltation.

The beloved John taught that when Christ appears in his glory, "we shall be like him; for we shall see him as he is. [We shall be pure] even as he is pure." (1 John 3:2-3.) And Paul adds that Jesus "being in the form of God, thought it not robbery to be equal with God." (Philippians 2:6.) It is thus clear in New Testament doctrine that men and women may be like the Father and the Son. When Jesus talked about becoming perfect as our Father in heaven is, he meant what he said.

To enjoy the quality of life that God enjoys, men and women must "enter into this order of the priesthood [meaning the new and everlasting covenant of marriage]." (D&C 131:2.) Part of the requirement of obtaining the divine nature is to participate in the ordinances of salvation and exaltation that God has participated in. The crowning ordinance is celestial marriage.

The revelation on marriage was given through Joseph Smith and recorded in 1843. In it the Lord said:

> I reveal unto you a new and an everlasting covenant; . . . all who will have a blessing at my hands shall abide the law which was appointed for that blessing. . . . If a man marry him a

wife . . . and he marry her not by me . . . their covenant and marriage are not of force when they are dead. . . . They are . . . appointed angels in heaven. . . . For these angels did not abide my law; therefore, they cannot be enlarged, but remain separately and singly, without exaltation, in their saved condition, to all eternity; and from henceforth are not gods, but are angels of God forever and ever.

And again . . . if a man marry a wife by my word, which is my law, . . . and if ye abide in my covenant, . . . it shall . . . be of full force when they are out of the world; and they shall pass by the angels . . . to their exaltation and glory . . . , which glory shall be a fulness and a continuation of the seeds forever and ever.

Then shall they be gods, because they have no end; therefore shall they be from everlasting to everlasting, because they continue; then shall they be above all, because all things are subject unto them. Then shall they be gods, because they have all power, and the angels are subject unto them. . . .

For strait is the gate, and narrow the way that leadeth unto the exaltation and continuation of the lives, and few there be that find it, because ye receive me not in the world, neither do ye know me.

But, if ye receive me in the world, then shall ye know me, and shall receive your exaltation; that where I am ye shall be also.

This is eternal lives — to know the only wise and true God, and Jesus Christ, whom he hath sent. I am he. Receive ye, therefore, my law. (D&C 132:4-24.)

In this monumental revelation we are given definition to the great Christian hope of becoming "joint-heirs with Christ . . . that we may be also glorified together." (Romans 8:17.) The fulfillment of this righteous hope within us is to become gods, even as he is God. The revelation defines godhood. It says "gods" (1) "have no end" and are "from everlasting to everlasting"; (2) are "above all, because all things are subject unto them"; (3) have "all power"; (4) enjoy "exaltation and continuation of the lives." (D&C 132:20, 22.) This is what Jesus has, and this is what those who are his heirs shall have. The great Christian hope is to be like Jesus our Lord God.

In the revelation the term *gods* refers to both men and women; that is, the wife and the husband who enter into and abide by this covenant and law together become gods. In this sense our mother in heaven is a god by scriptural definition. She enjoys the continuation of seeds and of the lives. Being a celestial parent is an essential characteristic of godhood. This is why in 1909 the First Presidency of the Church confidently talked of men and women coming from a "universal Father and Mother, and [being] literally the sons and daughters of Deity." The statement continues on to say: "Man is the child of God, formed in the divine image and endowed with divine attributes, and even as the infant son of an earthly father and mother is capable in due time of becoming a man, so the undeveloped offspring of celestial parentage is capable, by experience through ages and aeons, of evolving into a God." (Quoted in Joseph Fielding Smith, *Man: His Origin and Destiny*, pages 351, 355.)

Latter-day Saints believe that the final destiny for righteous women who observe gospel covenants, as with men of the same degree of faith and works, is godhood; that is, they may enjoy the same type and quality of life that the God of heaven now enjoys. This is fulfillment in the ultimate sense.

Thus we may conclude that in all the essential characteristics, the attributes which determine one's allegiance to righteousness and thus one's eternal reward, men and women are on an equal footing. Whether man or woman, one may accept or reject gospel principles, and regardless of sex the results of the choice will be identical in the hereafter. We may say then, that men and women are indeed equal in the sight of the Lord, that they are equal *in everything that counts.*

This is not to say that the difference in the roles will ever be erased. Clearly, it will not. Obviously, since God-ordained earthly patterns are reflections of heavenly ones, the priesthood holder will continue to preside in the exalted partnership throughout the eternities, while the woman likewise will fill in perfected form roles similar to those she knew on earth. Clearly, this must be the way it is with our celestial parents.

In today's world, of course, all this is not understood. Some people press for a so-called "equality" which nature has decreed as impossible, when the goal should really be equity in an accepted context of different roles for men and women. Thus feminists urge the surrender of preferential treatment for women (e.g. in property rights, alimony, support money) in favor of the doctrinaire slogan of "equality under the law." They confuse identical treatment with equal treatment, whereas there is such a condition as different but equal.

Males bear the priesthood. Females benefit from the administration of the priesthood. There is a difference. In this responsibility, the male bears much the greater burden. This, too, is a fact of life. It is a matter of divine designation of duties. The eligibility is set from on high — indeed, like the role of the wife and mother, it seems to be a part of the very fabric of eternity — and is not a fit subject for temporal legislation or argument.

I do not believe that bearing the priesthood is a greater or lesser assignment than that of bearing children and rearing them. But it is a responsibility to be filled. The man has a different job description than does the woman.

And the difference has no necessary relation to the relative attributes of the husband and wife. The respective degrees of intelligence, leadership qualities, or other abilities do not change the priesthood or childbearing roles. This is to say, if a woman is married to a man who does not have the ability or desire to magnify his calling by using his priesthood, the wife may be deprived of some priesthood blessings, but even in those circumstances she cannot usurp his position. She cannot, so to speak, put her hands on her own head and give herself a blessing. Such a wife may need to gently help her husband learn how to lead, how to use his priesthood in her behalf and in behalf of the family.

The wife who presides over her husband — who tells him where to work, where to live, how to live, and what to do — cannot reasonably suppose that he will take upon himself the obligations of priesthood service. Similarly, a husband who dominates his wife — who controls the finances, who insists on fashioning all significant decisions without consultation with his spouse, and who dictates to her — will create either a rebellious or a weak and unfulfilling marriage partner.

Some women must help their husbands assume the role of full partner in the marriage relationship. Likewise it is the lot of some husbands to magnify and enlarge their wives into equal partners.

That is what wives are supposed to be — equal partners. As we have stressed in this book, the meaningful dimension of equality is a proper expectation for men and women alike. Every spiritual attainment and future reward that is available to a good man is certainly available to a good woman.

It is my testimony that, as with righteous men, perfect peace and a full endowment of all good graces attend wives, mothers and daughters who are obedient to the laws of the gospel. These are celestial laws. Latter-day Saint women may enjoy in this life much of the promised joy, love, and charity. A fullness of these qualities is reserved for them — as joint heirs with their husbands — as members of exalted families in the heavens.

And as a pleasant reminder of the basic equality between a man and a woman, God has ordained that neither can attain the eternal heights without the other.

Index

Jacket art by Paul Mann
Book composed by Column Type
in Palatino and Palatino Italic
Printed by Publishers Press
on 60# Simpson Antique
Bound by Mountain States Bindery
in Sturdetan "40088" White, Goat